For Tim and Anne
With much love and affection,

Ken Gire

D1052944

Cañon City Public Library
Cañon City, Colorado

THE
NORTH FACE
of GOD

Hope for the times when God seems indifferent

KEN GIRE

Tyndale House Publishers, Inc.
, ILLINOIS

Visit Tyndale's exciting Web site at www.tyndale.com

TYNDALE is a registered trademark of Tyndale House Publishers, Inc.

Tyndale's quill logo is a trademark of Tyndale House Publishers, Inc.

The North Face of God

Copyright © 2005 by Reflective Living. All rights reserved.

Cover photograph copyright © by Gavin Hellier/Getty Images. All rights reserved.

Designed by Alyssa Force

Edited by Dave Lindstedt

Published in association with the literary agency of Alive Communications, Inc.,
7680 Goddard Street, Suite 200, Colorado Springs, CO 80920.

Unless otherwise indicated, all Scripture quotations are taken from the *Holy Bible,* New Living
Translation, copyright © 1996, 2004. Used by permission of Tyndale House Publishers, Inc.,
Wheaton, Illinois 60189. All rights reserved.

Scripture quotations marked NASB are taken from the *New American Standard Bible,*
© 1960, 1962, 1963, 1968, 1971, 1972, 1973, 1975, 1977 by The Lockman Foundation.
Used by permission.

Library of Congress Cataloging-in-Publication Data

Gire, Ken.
  The north face of God : hope for times when God seems indifferent / Ken Gire.
     p. cm.
  Includes bibliographical references.
  ISBN-10: 0-8423-7103-6 (hc)
  ISBN-13: 978-0-8423-7103-2 (hc)
  ISBN-10: 0-8423-7104-4 (sc)
  ISBN-13: 978-0-8423-7104-9 (sc)
  1. Consolation. 2. Hidden god. 3. Hope—Religious aspects—Christianity. I. Title.
  BV4909.G56 2005
  248.8′6—dc22   2005003416

Printed in the United States of America

11 10 09 08 07 06 05
 7   6   5   4   3   2   1

DEDICATED TO

Byron Gossett

He was a junior at TCU when I first met him,

two years ahead of me, a lowly freshman.

I looked up to him so much.

We played intramural basketball together.

He became my friend and later my roommate.

Although our bodies are too old now to play much basketball,

and although we now have different roommates,

he will always be my friend.

And I will always be looking up to him.

MAN
RAISES
HIMSELF
TOWARD
GOD
BY THE
QUESTIONS
HE ASKS
HIM.

Night by
Elie Wiesel

CONTENTS

ACKNOWLEDGMENTS

Thanks to everyone in my family for all the sacrifices they make so I can do the work I do. Especially to Judy, who ignores my tenement slum of books and papers for months at a time. And to my grandkids, who live with us, Samantha, Caleb, and Logan: I can come out and play now!

Thanks to Ron Beers, who embraced this project when it was little more than a title and subtitle. Thanks to Ken Petersen, who shepherded the manuscript with great sensitivity. And thanks to Dave Lindstedt, my editor. If Jesus had been an editor instead of a carpenter, I think he would have approached his work and his relationships with authors a lot like Dave does.

Thanks to the three men I interviewed for this project: "Jim," "David," and Darrell. Their stories were painful for them to tell and painful for me to write. They are brave and good men. And I am a better person because of them.

Thanks to the "Chetter Group" for their friendship, for their kindness to my family, and for giving me a refreshing break from the pressures of writing this book.

Thanks to the woman who attended one of my seminars and was kind enough to send me the book of Thornton Wilder's plays, which I quote from in this book. I'm sorry for not remembering your name, but I do remember your kindness.

Thanks to Howard Brooks, a skilled mountain climber, who read the manuscript to check the accuracy of my research.

Thanks to Judy Mikalonis for her "scoopage" and "snackage," but more importantly for her friendship and her prayers for this project.

Thanks to the board of Reflective Living: Mark Weaver, Darnell Boehm, and Roc Bottomly. Thank you for loving me and my family and for helping me be a better steward of my life.

Thanks to Randy Wolff for letting me sequester myself at Wind

River Ranch in Estes Park, Colorado, to work and think and pray my way through a difficult impasse in the writing of this book.

And finally: The difference between a pretty good book and a really good book is Lee Hough. Special thanks to him—my friend, my agent, my brother-in-law. He has been the first reader and finest critic for a number of my books, and never more than for this one.

INTRODUCTION

Has the Lord rejected me forever?
Will he never again be kind to me?
Is his unfailing love gone forever?
Have his promises permanently failed?
Has God forgotten to be gracious?
Has he slammed the door on his compassion?

PSALM 77:7-9

FROM OUR VANTAGE POINT, the span of biblical history seems a range of majestic peaks silhouetted against the horizon. I wonder, though, how majestic that terrain seemed to those who first traversed it.

Consider Joseph. When his brothers betrayed him, tossed him into a pit, and then sold him into slavery, I wonder how providential it felt. How near did God seem from the bottom of the cistern of circumstances into which Joseph was thrown? What caravan of questions and doubts traveled with him all the way to Egypt? What clang of confusion arose in the prison where the accusations of Potiphar's wife sent him?

Who knows for sure? The biblical record is silent.

But it is not silent in the case of Job. Although he emerged from the avalanche of events that had buried him with his eternal perspective still intact, the shivering senselessness of the avalanche soon overtook him. Feeling attacked by his friends and abandoned by God, he pleaded for a hearing in heaven, demanding his day in court, where his case could be tried and a verdict decided once and for all. His questions were as raw as his wounds, and as unstaunchable.

Neither is the record silent regarding David. His questions cry out from caves in the wilderness, where he hid at different times from Saul, Absalom, and the Philistines, among others. Yet, regardless of how hard he squinted, David sometimes couldn't see so much as a shadow of God's presence flitting over the sun-scorched terrain. Regardless of how hard he strained, he often couldn't hear so much as a syllable of God's voice echoing through the stone-carved canyons. It didn't make sense. Why was God so near to him in the palace, yet so far from him in the wilderness?

For these characters in biblical history, the silence was likely more confusing than their suffering, and the abandonment they felt more painful than their affliction.

In our own experience with God, at some time or another, we have all encountered the silence of heaven. Many of us have felt abandoned by God. And we have known the pain of unanswered questions.

Some have known this pain more than others, felt the abandonment more deeply, experienced the silence longer. Many have been persistent in praying for healing or wholeness or deliverance. Just as many have been passionate in praying for a parent or a mate or a child. And though these prayers were all made in faith, all motivated from the best of intentions, they have gone unanswered.

Unanswered questions can form an impasse in our relationship with God that is Himalayan in its expanse. Stopped there, we look to the highest mountain in that range, to the God we once knew—or thought we knew—and the God whose paternal arms we once felt wrapped so protectively around us now seems an Everest of indifference.

With that sudden sting of awareness comes a blizzard of questions.

Amid the blizzard, as we stand there in the shivering cold, we sometimes lose our bearings, and we wonder:

Did we ever feel the arms of a heavenly Father around us? Or was it just a break in the weather and a patch of sudden sun upon our skin?

Were the answers we once heard the sound of his voice? Or was it simply the sound of our own voices echoing off the cliffs?

Was he always like this, and the wispy clouds of our spiritual imagination merely obscured that reality? Or did he somehow change?

And did we do something to cause that change?

Or was it something we failed to do?

Climbing Mount Everest is a metaphor of our pursuit of God to find answers to our most searching questions. Everest has different faces, each of which has been climbed by various expeditions over the past century. The North Face of Everest can be the most technically difficult to climb because it is the side of the mountain that generally receives the least snowfall, forcing climbers to scale bare rock.

For many who are suffering, God seems distant, cold, and strangely silent. And when we come to him with our questions, it seems we are climbing the North Face of Mount Everest, scaling unstable rock.

We climb in hopes of reaching some summit of understanding. But the air is thin, the heights are dizzying, and clouds are everywhere, hemming us in at every turn.

Some find their faith on that climb.

Others lose it, forever numb to the feelings they once had for God.

The risks are real. Only a novice would dismiss them. The more experienced climbers stand at the base of the mountain, sobered by those realities. Yet something draws them up the mountain.

One day or another, you and I will likely gather at the same base camp, sobered by those same realities. And there we will face a choice.

We can stay where we are, huddled in our tents, warming ourselves as best we can.

Or . . .

With ice axes in hand, we can scale what seems to be the North Face of God to find answers to our most searching questions.

In this book I tell the stories of three men who have made that climb, each of them by a different route that was determined by the losses they experienced. I tell lesser stories, too, but not of lesser losses. They are lesser only in the way that minor chords are to major chords in musical composition. Together they make up the deep and somber notes of a symphony of sorrows. As you listen to those notes, I pray they will not only resonate with your own sorrows but also give rest to your sorrows with ever-rising refrains of hope.

For a subject as complex as the silence of God in the face of our suffering, this book is hardly the last word. It is more like the first word, a starting place for those who hurt. It's not a travel manual; it's a traveling companion.

I hope its words are true, its voice is kind, and it proves to be good company for the climb.

A PRAYER BEFORE CLIMBING

Dear Lord,

We have lived so much of our lives on the foothills of spiritual experience,
  enjoying the view in safety and comfort,
    warming ourselves by the fires of other people's stories.

But those fires have embered away
  and no longer warm us the way they used to.

We need our own stories and the warmth that they bring. We want to know you,
Lord, not just know about you.

We don't need another Bible study.
  We need you.

So we leave this sedentary life behind and climb to higher ground
  in hopes that there we might find you.

The once-distant theological peaks are now jaggedly personal.

And so we ask you to grant us some foothold upon which we can steady ourselves,
  some handhold from which we can raise ourselves higher.

We have never walked this way before,
  this very dangerous, mountain way,
    and we are afraid.

Afraid of what we may find there.

Afraid of what we may not.

Grant us traveling mercies for the climb, Lord.

Though our steps be slow, grant they be sure.

Though our progress be slight, grant it be steady.

We will look to the mountains as David did,
  trusting that you are our help
    and that you will not let us stumble or fall.

For you know how bad our knees are,
  how weak our lungs,
    and how afraid we are of heights.

CHAPTER ONE

ASCENDING WITH OUR INITIAL QUESTIONS

How long, O Lord, will you look on and do nothing?

PSALM 35:17

MOUNT EVEREST sits enthroned in the Himalayan mountain range, an alpine uplift formed eons ago by the collision of two continents. At 29,035 feet, its summit is the highest spot on earth, and still rising. As a mountain, it is in its adolescence, adding a quarter of an inch every year as the tectonic plates beneath it continue to push upward.

Its pyramid-like formation separates the northern border of India from China, and if you fell to the right from one of its ridges, it is possible that you would drop eight thousand feet into Chinese-controlled Tibet; if you fell to the left, you would fall six thousand feet into Nepal. Known to those who live in its shadow as Chomolungma, "Goddess Mother of the World," the mountain was renamed after Sir George Everest, British director of the nineteenth-century Great Trigonometrical Survey of India.

Over the years a number of statistics have been compiled of Everest expeditions. Two records are most notable: those who have reached the summit and those who have died trying.

Some have died from medical conditions: dehydration, hypoxia, hypothermia, and pulmonary and cerebral edema. Some climbers simply fell asleep and never woke up. A number have died in avalanches, others from a disorienting temporary blindness that stranded them without hope of rescue. Still others died from sudden storms with winds up to ninety miles an hour. Most, however, lost their footing and fell to their deaths.

Tibetan peasants living at the base of the mountain offer prayers so that climbers won't lose their footing and fall. They do this by burning juniper twigs and putting out prayer flags—brightly colored squares of fabric on which prayers are printed—strung together like laundry hung out to dry. These Tibetan Buddhists believe that the flags hold the prayers of the climbers, which, when blown by the wind, ascend to the goddess of the mountain, bringing blessing on the expedition.

Often, our own prayers, especially those we pray when we're young, are similarly simple: seeking God's blessings. Or they are prayers of gratitude, thanking God for the dew-dropped wonder of the world we live in—a world full of sunshine, or at least rainbows amid the rain.

But then one day something happens. Clouds rush in, riding on gale-force winds that threaten to blow you off the mountain. You learn that you have cancer or that your spouse is having an affair or your child has been arrested or your best friend betrays you. Suddenly, the world in all its wonder doesn't seem so wonderful anymore. The clouds cluster low and unbroken, unrelenting. The fury of the tempest seems so personal, and it's all you can do to hunker down and hang on.

God, we are told, mercifully causes the rain to fall upon the just and the unjust. Most of us can understand that, even children. When it comes to floods, though—or tsunamis—it's a little more difficult to understand. When the harsh realities of life sweep over the serenity of our relationship with God, the aftermath of that torrential downpour can be devastating. Like the devastation that came to a friend of mine named Lee. Hear his prayer as he wrestled with God's silence during a painful period of unemployment:

> *God help me, please!*
>
> *Please don't humiliate me again,*
>
> *not before my friends*
>
> *not before my wife*

not before my children

not before my parents. . . .

*Father, what's helping find me a job compared to the power it takes
You to run this world for even one day?*

Nothing!

*If a sparrow doesn't fall without You noticing, why aren't You
noticing me? Why are You tending millions of beautiful flowers that
bloom today and are gone tomorrow but You won't tend to me, Your
child? One nod, one word from You and a door would open. Why
are You humiliating me?. . .*

*Jesus, I don't know any more words. I have no more words. Does
Your silence mean, No, You won't help? Does it mean, wait?*

How long?

I'm listening, Lord. Straining to hear.

*I'm calling, Lord, with all my heart. Please, let me laugh again, help
me find my reason for getting up in the mornings, take away this
humiliation that slaps me in the face all day, every day.*

During Lee's time of unemployment, I also prayed. His disappointment with God became mine. It hurt so much to see him hurt. I could offer him a lot of things—my friendship, my encouragement, my prayers—but I couldn't offer him the one thing he needed. And it wasn't a job. It was a connection with God, a God he felt no longer cared enough to listen, let alone to speak or to help.

Below is the prayer of a woman who feels just as helpless in regard to a friend of hers. The prayer is by Patricia Hooper and first appeared in *The Atlantic Monthly* magazine.

> *Lord, I call to you—*
> *there is someone*
> *I want you to follow home.*

The night is cold.
The wet leaves hide the edges
of the dark path. He
is lost. I would
go with him if I could,
put my arms around him,
share my coat. He is
three hundred miles
away. No one else
sees him. Do you
see him, his step hurried
through the black rain?
Or are you
still busy, as you were when,
before he harmed himself
the last time, he was the one
who called?

Can you hear the slosh of the lonely footsteps? Can you feel the numbness of the face blotched with cold? Can you sense the desperation of the man who once called to God but calls to him no longer?

Are you still busy?

There is an indictment in the question—subtle but unmistakable. The indictment is stronger in the following prayer, pressing its litigious finger against the chest of a God who seems to be hiding behind his Fifth Amendment rights.

The prayer is from a journal entry in *Lament for a Son*, a father's attempt to reach a summit of understanding about the death of his son. The son's name was Eric. The father is Nicholas Wolterstorff. If anyone should have been equipped with the right questions for such a climb, it would be Wolterstorff, a professor of philosophical theology at Yale Divinity School. Yet neither an institution as pedigreed as Yale, nor a career as prestigious as teaching, nor a field as profound as theology, was able to give this grieving father the answers he was searching for.

Eric was bright, and his future was full of promise. He entered college as a National Merit Scholar, excelling in math, science, and computer programming and majoring in art history. He was an accomplished artist and musician who traveled extensively and lived life to the fullest. Mountains were his passion. He loved the beauty, the solitude. He loved the challenge of the climb and the exhilaration of the heights. He loved it all, to the very end.

Eric was twenty-five when one misstep on an Austrian mountainside cost him his life. His death devastated the family, especially his father, who worked through his grief one slippery step at a time, hacking away at the ice with his questions in an attempt to gain a foothold of comprehension. He first asked himself the questions, then he asked his family, his friends, and finally God.

> *How is faith to endure, O God, when you allow all this scraping and tearing on us? You have allowed rivers of blood to flow, mountains of suffering to pile up, sobs to become humanity's song—all without lifting a finger that we could see. You have allowed bonds of love beyond number to be painfully snapped. If you have not abandoned us, explain yourself.*

Every time I watch the nightly news, it seems that somewhere in the world a new river of blood begins to flow. Some sudden upthrust of suffering unsettles the landscape. Some newly saddened refrain reaches for heaven, but its trembling hands go begging, the way they did one night while I was working on this book.

The evening news included a story about a kidnapping in a small town in North Dakota. A woman had been abducted as she was walking to her car in the parking lot of the shopping mall where she worked. Her name was Dru Sjodin. She was twenty-two.

At the time, two of my daughters were twenty-one and twenty-four. They also worked at a mall, also walked to their cars in the parking lot. *Thank God they are safe*, I remember thinking. "*Keep* them safe, God, please," I remember praying.

I prayed for the woman who'd been kidnapped. I prayed for her every day, several times a day. Who knows how many others prayed? Thousands, hundreds of thousands, perhaps millions. I prayed for

▲

Dru until I heard that her blood had been found in a sex offender's car, along with a knife in the trunk that also had her blood on it. My heart sank along with my hope. Five months later, as I was writing these pages, I heard that her body had been found.

I cried. I got angry. I got depressed.

Suddenly God seemed less sovereign, the world less certain, our lives less safe. And a family was left shattered—forever. Life for them will never be the same. A part of them will always be wounded, always be sad, always empty. That moment of tragedy will forever leech color from every other moment in their lives—not just the moments that lie ahead of them but also all that lie behind, for the happiness they once felt is forever altered by the sadness of all that was lost, all that was cut short, all that will never be.

If God is everywhere present, he saw what happened in that car. If God is all powerful, he could have stopped it. That he saw it and did nothing to stop it is the darkest and most unsettling mystery in the universe.

From that black hole in our otherwise orderly system of theology comes a densely packed array of questions. Why, God? Why was this young woman's life cut short? And why was it cut short in such a tragic way? Why didn't you intervene? Why do you allow such horrendous evil in the world? Why don't you put your foot down and put a stop to it? Why don't you *make* your will be done here on earth as it is in heaven?

Why, God? Why?

▲ ▲ ▲

When questions like that go unanswered, it feels as if God has abandoned us. And if he hasn't abandoned us, we feel he at least owes us an explanation for his silence. That is the heart of Jesus' prayer on the cross: "My God, my God, why have you abandoned me?" How painful a question for the Son of that God to ask.

He doesn't ask, "Why are the soldiers treating me like this?"
He knows why: They know not what they are doing.

8

He doesn't ask, "Why did Peter deny me?"
  He knows why: Satan had demanded to sift him like wheat.

He doesn't ask, "Why am I being crucified?"
  He knows why: It is for this reason that he came to this world.

Jesus could bear the pain of the nails, the thorns, the beatings. He could bear the public humiliation, the personal ridicule. He could bear the betrayal, the desertion, the denial of his friends. But the abandonment of God he could not bear.

We are told that before Jesus raised that anguished question, he was shrouded in three hours of darkness. Who knows all that he endured during those hours. Who knows how much physical pain he endured, how much psychological pain, how much spiritual pain. Who knows what access the forces of darkness had to him, to his mind, his emotions, even to his dreams as he drifted in and out of consciousness. All we know is that at the end of those three hours he "called out with a loud voice" (Matthew 27:46).

The words he called out are from the first verse of Psalm 22, a psalm of lament voiced by David a thousand years earlier:

> *My God, my God, why have you*
> *abandoned me?*
> *Why are you so far away?*

I think of that last question, and a bumper sticker comes to mind. You've seen it, I'm sure: *If God seems distant, guess who moved?*

How would you like to follow *that* car to church?

How would you like to be in a small group with the driver?

Or share a table at Starbucks?

How do you feel when the pain of your struggle is reduced to a slogan? Worse still, a sarcastic slogan. When we are hurting, we need sensitivity, not sarcasm; a listening ear, not a lecture; a place where we can lay down our burdens, not a platitude to add onto them.

> If God seems distant, guess who moved?
> *Had David moved?*

Read his next words in Psalm 22 and decide for yourself:
> *Every day I call to you, my God, but you do not answer.*
> *Every night you hear my voice, but I find no relief.*

From the context of the psalm, we know that David's life hung in the balance (vv. 20-21). His circumstances were never more desperate, yet his God never more distant. Had David moved? It doesn't sound like it. It sounds as if he sought God day and night.

Had Nicholas Wolterstorff moved when he questioned God about the death of his son? Had Patricia Hooper moved when she questioned God's care for her friend? Had Lee Hough moved?

Had Jesus?

Had you, when during the most agonizing time of your life you called out to God, and he was silent?

So how do you reconcile a God who cares with a God who doesn't speak, doesn't seem to act, doesn't seem to lift even a finger in the face of such desperate circumstances? The feeding of a family that is starving for some crust of hope. The protection of a suicidal friend. The saving of a son who has fallen down a mountain.

What makes it more difficult to reconcile is that he is not only our God, but also our Father. And Jesus not only told us to pray to him (Matthew 6:9-13), he told us what to expect from him: "You parents—if your children ask for a loaf of bread, do you give them a stone instead? Or if they ask for a fish, do you give them a snake? Of course not! So if you sinful people know how to give good gifts to your children, how much more will your heavenly Father give good gifts to those who ask him" (Matthew 7:9-11).

What should a child do when he asks his father for something to eat, and the father hands him a snake? Can we blame him for jumping back with an astonished look on his face? It is only right for the child to raise a question, calling out in a loud voice, "Why? Why would you do such a thing? You're my father. I thought you loved me. I thought you cared for me. I thought I could come to you for anything."

The only way a child can gain understanding of such a circumstance is if he asks honest and heartfelt questions.

Tibetan Buddhism teaches its adherents to avoid the stress that strong emotions bring—to avoid the disappointment, the anger, and the despair that loss may bring. Yet it seems that by denying these emotions we are denying our humanity.

How can one be human and *not* have strong emotions in the face of heart-wrenching losses? And how can those emotions not raise questions?

Our prayers are not something we string out to flap in the wind, hoping a sudden gust lifts our words to some benevolent deity. They are so much more substantial. They are full of wonder and gratitude, curiosity and concern, joy and sorrow.

And questions.

From the Edenic innocence of our childhood prayers to the east-of-Eden prayers of our adulthood, we raise ourselves to God by the questions we ask. That was the opinion of Moshe, the religious mentor of Elie Wiesel, a young Jewish boy who grew up in Moshe's neighborhood and became a prolific author, a celebrated academic, and winner of the Nobel Peace Prize.

> *"Man raises himself toward God by the questions he asks Him," he was fond of repeating. "That is the true dialogue. Man questions God and God answers. But we don't understand His answers. We can't understand them. Because they come from the depths of the soul, and stay there until death. . . ."*

> *"And why do you pray, Moshe?" I asked him.*

> *"I pray . . . that He will give me the strength to ask Him the right questions."*

A PRAYER FOR UNDERSTANDING

Lord,

I know that an overwhelming majority of people pray. Even atheists pray some of the time. And when the fate of a loved one is at stake, everyone prays.

Yet in spite of our prayers, not all of our loved ones make it off the mountain. Some fall to their deaths. Some fall sick and die. Some fall prey to freezing weather.

So what makes the difference?

Good equipment? Good balance? Or is it just good luck?

And how does prayer fit into it all?

People pray and live. People pray and die.

Is it some formula that makes the difference? Some special wording? What?

I know you care about what happens here in this world. You created it. You sustain it. You sent your Son to die for it.

So why don't you intervene more often? Why don't you respond more quickly—especially when the prayers are so urgent?

I sometimes feel like a child in a world that has lost its wonder,
*   in a world that has turned scary with shadows,*
*   and I can't find my way home.*

Please be patient with all my questions,
*   especially with the ones that seem so childish.*

And grant that in my faltering prayers
*   I might stumble across a question*
*   that leads me closer to you.*

base camp

▲

Altitude: 17,700 Feet

For the choir director: A psalm of David.

O LORD, how long will you forget me?
Forever?
How long will you look the other way?
How long must I struggle with anguish in my soul,
with sorrow in my heart every day?
How long will my enemy have the upper hand?

Turn and answer me, O LORD my God!
Restore the sparkle to my eyes,
or I will die.
Don't let my enemies gloat, saying, "We have
defeated him!"
Don't let them rejoice at my downfall.

But I trust in your unfailing love.
I will rejoice because you have rescued me.
I will sing to the LORD
because he is good to me.
PSALM 13

In climbing Mount Everest by the route taken by Sir Edmund Hillary and Tenzing Norgay, the first climbers to successfully reach the summit, everyone starts at the same place.

Base Camp.

Base Camp is located at the bottom of the Khumbu Glacier. There the climbing team assembles to take inventory of its supplies, check the equipment for a final time, discuss strategy, and be examined by the expedition's doctor to make sure everyone is physically ready for the ascent. The ascent from Base Camp to the summit takes a couple of months, so several camps are necessary along the way for the climbing teams to rest, rehydrate, and acclimatize before they ascend to the next level.

In the course of this book, I would like to take a similar approach, pausing at some strategic places to allow you time to rest and reflect before we go on to the next chapter. The 1953 route taken by Edmund Hillary and Tenzing Norgay had a total of nine camps, and that will be the same number we will use in our own ascent.

Because climbers are sometimes snowed in for days at a time, they often bring a book to read. On the historic 1924 expedition of George Mallory and Andrew Irvine, for example, when they were in their tent at the various camps, they read poetry to each other from Robert Bridge's anthology, *The Spirit of Man*, and talked about its meaning.

Instead of selections of poetry, I would like us to read selections from the Psalms. And I would like us to talk about them, particularly how they relate to us when God seems an Everest of indifference.

▲ ▲ ▲

Psalm 13, quoted at the beginning of this section, is the first psalm we will consider. The superscription tells us it was written by David. I don't know what circumstances prompted his prayer, but from the context, he is at an impasse in his relationship with God, struggling for a foothold. His enemies are overwhelming him, and that is part of what he is struggling with, but that struggle is not nearly as great as the enigma of God's seeming indifference. "How long?" becomes the refrain of his lament, which he repeats four times:

> *O LORD, how long will you forget me?*
> *. . . How long will you look the other way?*
> *How long must I struggle with anguish in my soul,*
> *with sorrow in my heart every day?*
> *How long will my enemy have the upper hand?*
> *(vv. 1-2)*

With these questions he chips away at the ice, trying to cut a step or secure a piton* that will take him closer to a summit of understanding. It appears, though, that he is suffering from spiritual snow blindness and is in danger of falling headlong down the mountain.

> *Turn and answer me, O LORD my God!*
> *Restore the sparkle to my eyes, or I will die. (v. 3)*

Some kind of downfall appears imminent, but before he loses his footing, he looks at the rope around his waist, which grows taut and holds him. That rope is one of the great characteristics of God.

> *But I trust in your* unfailing *love.*
> *(v. 5, emphasis mine)*

The phrase "unfailing love" comes from a single Hebrew word: *chesed.* It is a word particularly used in contexts of God's love for his people. The love is not only initiated by him but also sustained by him. It emphasizes the faithfulness of God's love over generations in spite of how wayward the object of his love is in any given generation.

David's own waywardness is a case in point, as seen in Psalm 25:6-7:

> *Remember, O LORD, your compassion and unfailing love,*
> *which you have shown from long ages past.*
> *Do not remember the rebellious sins of my youth.*
> *Remember me in the light of your unfailing love,*
> *for you are merciful, O LORD.*

Later in David's life, when he committed adultery with Bathsheba and arranged to have her husband killed, he again appealed to God. But not on the basis of his position as king; or of his personal merit;

*For definitions of mountain-climbing terms see the glossary at the end of the book.

or of his past accomplishments, such as his slaying of Goliath. Notice the appeal in Psalm 51:

> *Have mercy on me, O God,*
> because *of your unfailing love. (v. 1, emphasis mine)*

So confident was David in this characteristic of God that it was also the basis of his hope for the future.

> *Surely your goodness and unfailing love*
> *will pursue me all the days of my life,*
> *and I will live in the house of the LORD forever. (Psalm 23:6)*

I don't know where you are on the mountain or what put you there. I don't know how wearied you are by the climb or how weathered you are by the elements. I don't know how alone or abandoned you feel. I don't know how disoriented you are or how despondent. But wherever you are and however you feel, I want you to curl up in your tent . . . close your eyes . . . and remember.

Remember your own history with God, the way David remembered his. Think back on the times when God expressed his love for you. Remember those times? Remember the words he spoke? Remember the way he answered your prayers? Remember the gifts he gave you? the many kindnesses he showed you? the forgiveness? the protection? Remember the love you felt for him, the joy, the tears? Remember how he touched you, embraced you, and led you?

He hasn't changed. Neither has his love for you. It may not *seem* to be there, the way a rope around your waist doesn't seem to be there when it's slack. But it *is* there. Paul told us that nothing— nothing—would ever be able separate us from the love of God that is revealed in Christ Jesus (Romans 8:35-39).

God's love for us, not ours for him, is the rope around our waist.

It's a rope that doesn't fray, no matter how much it is stretched.

It doesn't freeze, no matter how cold it gets.

It doesn't fail, no matter how far we fall . . . or how often.

A PRAYER OF GRATITUDE

Dear God,

Thank you for the base camps you have placed in my life.

Thank you for the time to rest and recuperate from the rigors of the climb.

Thank you for the opportunity to get rehydrated from your Word.

Thank you for allowing me whatever time I need to adjust to the altitude.

How monotonous it must seem to you—all the "How longs?" that I have prayed.

But, Lord, how I want the snow to stop and the poor visibility that goes with it.

How I want the wind to stop and the cold that goes with it.

How I want the burning in my lungs to stop,
*   the soreness in my legs,*
*   the dizziness in my head.*

Hold on to me, Lord.

Hold on to me with the rope of your unfailing love,
*   for the slope ahead seems so steep,*
*   the steps so slippery,*
*   and the summit so far away.*

Help me to trust not the strength of my legs in making the climb,
*   but the strength of your arms holding the other end of the rope.*

Keep my eyes, not on how slack that rope may seem at the moment,
*   but simply on the next step that lies ahead of me.*

What is that next step, Lord?

One step, that's all I ask. Just show me that one step.
*   And once it is clear, give me the courage to take it.*

With each step I will trust in your unfailing love
*   to hold me, to guide me, and to keep me safe.*

CHAPTER TWO

FINDING AN ACCURATE MAP

Come quickly, LORD, and answer me,
for my depression deepens.
Don't turn away from me,
or I will die.
Let me hear of your unfailing love
each morning,
for I am trusting you.
Show me where to walk,
for I give myself to you.

PSALM 143:7-8

T HE EARLIEST RENDERINGS
of Mount Everest were simple sketches. Later the landscape was
mapped by hand, using primitive instruments. Today the methods
of mapping are more sophisticated. The most recent measurement
of the mountain was done in 1999, using precise calculations made
possible by the millions of data points collected by the Space Shuttle
and the Global Positioning System.

With each generation, the map gets more accurate. And this is
how it should be, both in the natural realm and the spiritual realm.

It seems to me the responsibility of each generation is to map the
terrain of faith with ever-greater accuracy. We are not painting pictures for our children; we are making maps for climbers, which our
children will one day become. There are clefts in the rock where
they can find shelter, but there are also crevasses into which they can
fall to their deaths. To map the clefts and not the crevasses would be
unconscionable.

If I am going to put my life on the line in the journey of faith, and
if I am to ask others to do the same, I want a realistic map to guide my
steps, not an artist's rendering. And I don't want the jagged realities
softened with an air brush.

I have a contour map of Mount Everest, which is a flattened view
of the mountain with lines that mark the elevation. This type of map
is important because it lets climbers know what the altitude is at any
given place. It tells them how steep an incline they will be facing. Or

how precipitous a drop-off. That's important because a lot of scary things happen at high altitudes. The human body begins to break down, with disastrous consequences. Cerebral edema, for example, can lead to disorientation, even death. Oxygen deprivation can cause hallucinations, slow our steps, unsteady them, or misdirect them, sending us plunging down the slopes.

When the journey of faith becomes treacherous, we need an accurate map of the emotional terrain, because there will be a certain amount of spiritual disorientation along the way, some emotional vertigo, and more than a few hallucinations. The map that prepares us for the emotional ups and downs of our journey is the book of Psalms. The view is from a peak in one psalm, from a pit in another. The footing is sure one moment, shaky the next. The mood is joyful in one, sorrowful in another.

But here is where we have to be careful as spiritual cartographers. We pick and choose the psalms we want to read, the ones we want to adapt to music, the ones we want to preach on. As a result, some psalms, such as Psalm 23, get a lot of air time. Others, such as Psalm 22, do not. Yet as we make our way through the Psalms, we learn that life is not all green pastures and still waters. Although we are led there, we are not left there to live out our lives. We are led through wildernesses, we pass through shadowed valleys, and we are made to walk on high places, above the tree line. All are part of the landscape of faith.

▲ ▲ ▲

The Psalms were composed by a number of different songwriters, but the most prolific among them was King David. For generations, the lyrics of his life have inspired people of all ages. One of those people is Bono, lead singer of the band U2, who has been a fan of David's since the age of twelve. One of the reasons he was originally drawn to him was because of all the struggles the king had endured.

"He was forced into exile and ended up in a cave in some no-name border town facing the collapse of his ego and abandonment by God," Bono explains.

"But this is where the soap opera got interesting," Bono says, and you can almost see a glint in his eye as he says it. "This is where David was said to have composed his first psalm—a blues. That's what a lot of the psalms feel like to me, the blues. Man shouting at God—'My God, my God why hast thou forsaken me? Why art thou so far from helping me?' " (Psalm 22). The heart of Bono's own lyrics is remarkably similar to David's. And like David's psalms, his songs come from the everyday experiences of his life.

"A Beautiful Day," for example, is a hard-driving hymn of hope, pulsing with life, which Bono wrote in celebration of the $430 million dollars of debt that the U.S. canceled in loans to Africa, a cause he had been championing for years.

On the opposite end of the emotional spectrum is "Sunday, Bloody Sunday," a protest song against the cycle of violence between the Irish Republican Army and the British. "I can't believe the news today," the song begins. "I can't close my eyes and make it go away." And then the plaintive refrain: "How long? How long must we sing this song?" The lyrics capture the tenor of so many of the circumstances in which David found himself—surrounded by enemies who were threatening his life. The more recent "Peace on Earth" is a lament. It was written on a day when a bomb went off in the Irish town of Omagh, killing twenty-nine people and wounding numerous others. The lyrics reflect Bono's despair:

> Jesus, this song you wrote,
> The words are sticking in my throat,
> Peace on Earth.
> Hear it every Christmas time,
> But hope and history won't rhyme . . .
> Peace on Earth.

There are times when hope and history simply won't rhyme. How do you rhyme the Exodus with the Holocaust? Or Daniel in the lions' den with Christians in the Colosseum? They don't rhyme. And they won't rhyme, no matter how hard we try to force them.

The same could be said about our own hopes and our own history. Our hopes have such a strong musical cadence to them, whereas our history seems to have no metrical pattern at all, let alone any semblance of a rhyme scheme.

Bono's lyrics get to the heart of all humanity's dialogue with God. He goes on to sing:

> *Jesus, can you take the time*
> *To throw a drowning man a line?*
> *Peace on Earth.*

The lyrics are a contemporary version of some of the lyrics in the Psalms—and of some of the psalms in our own lives. Sometimes it seems it would take so little effort for Jesus to look our way and nod to a nearby angel to send us the word we so desperately need to hear. It would take so little time to throw us a line as we are thrashing about in the choppy waters that surround us, trying to keep our heads above water and gulping for air.

As Bono places the biblical refrain next to the verses of his life, you can't help but think of your own verses and how poorly they sometimes rhyme. Commenting on the lyrics and the real-life circumstances that inspired them, Bono said, "That Christmas, the whole 'peace on earth, goodwill to all men' struck a sour note. It was very hard to be a believer that Christmas."

There are times in our lives when it is hard being a Christian. Christmases when it's hard to be joyful. Thanksgivings when it's hard to be grateful. New Years when it's hard to be hopeful. Times when we feel disappointed with life, maybe even despairing of life. Times when we feel abandoned by God.

The Psalms that have themes of abandonment and displacement are some of Bono's favorites. He explains, "It's in his despair that the psalmist really reveals the nature of his special relationship with God." In our own relationship with God, there will doubtless be beautiful days and just as doubtless a few bloody Sundays. What Bono does so well is tell the truth about such days, both about the delight he feels and about the despair.

The honesty of Bono's lyrics is the honesty we see in the Psalms—and the kind of honesty we should see in our lives.

I don't see myself as a dishonest person, yet in a thousand different ways and on a thousand different days I am. For I have often kept my tears to myself, my confusion to myself—my misery, my brokenness, my desperation, and my loneliness to myself. And for what? For my own good? For the good of the children? my friends?

Why am I like that, I wonder? Why are so many of us like that?

I think it's because, in our pull-yourself-up-by-your-own-bootstraps culture, we are reluctant, perhaps even fearful, to admit we need help. In contrast to the independent spirit of our culture is the dependent spirit of the culture of our faith. "My help comes from the Lord," the psalmist proclaims (Psalm 121:2), and many of the Psalms are about our inability to help in any significant way with the pain and suffering we face in life.

When the help we find in ourselves runs out, we are ready for the Psalms.

Look at the prayers that are there. "Help me . . ." "Rescue me . . ." "Save me . . ." "Deliver me . . ."

Unbearable circumstances are the mysterious strangers who bring us to those kinds of prayers.

A PRAYER FOR HONESTY

Dear Lord,

Thank you for the Psalms,
*   especially the psalms of lament*
*   that map the geography of the heart*
*   with all its emotional peaks and valleys.*

Grant me traveling mercies for the terrain
*   you have ordained for me to walk.*

Give me songs for my journey, Lord,
*   songs that tell the truth about life in general*
*   and about my life in particular.*

Like Bono's songs. Like David's.

Help me to understand that honesty is what hones the edge of the ice ax,
*   and that without emotionally honest questions,*
*   I may traverse a lot of ground horizontally*
*   but make little progress vertically.*

camp ii

▲

Altitude: 19,400 Feet

But I trust in your unfailing love.
I will rejoice because you have rescued me.
I will sing to the LORD because he is good to me.
PSALM 13:5-6

You are my hiding place; you protect me from trouble.
You surround me with songs of victory.
PSALM 32:7

But each day the LORD pours his unfailing love upon me,
and through each night I sing his songs,
praying to God who gives me life.
PSALM 42:8

Unseal my lips, O Lord,
that my mouth may praise you.
PSALM 51:15

Then I will praise God's name with singing,
and I will honor him with thanksgiving.
PSALM 69:30

But you, O LORD, will sit on your throne forever,
Your fame will endure to every generation.
PSALM 102:12

Midway through the treacherous Khumbu Icefall we reach Camp II, where we climb into our tents, exhausted and needing to be rehydrated. Ice has to be melted to provide drinking water, and this time we will break off small chunks from a number of different psalms to provide the refreshment we need.

But first, let's consider some thoughts from Nicholas Wolterstorff's *Lament for a Son*.

When Wolterstorff turned to music for comfort, he found the songs too positive, too affirming. He looked for other music, this time a requiem, but he felt there was too little brokenness in it.

"Is there no music that *fits* our brokenness?" he asked himself.

Precious little, I would have to say in answer to that question. I know that when I went through depressing periods in my life— whether it was a protracted period of unemployment, a disorienting period of a child's rebellion, or an intense period of physical pain—I couldn't listen to popular music, either. It was too light, too joyful.

The collection of 150 psalms in our Bible was Israel's hymnbook. Included in the collection were joyful songs—songs of faith and hope, songs of praise and thanksgiving. But also included were sorrowful songs—songs of doubt and despair, songs of confusion and disillusionment. Somewhere in that collection is a song that understands, music that fits our brokenness. In contemporary Christian music, there are few such songs. Like the psalms quoted at the beginning of this chapter, there is praise in our songs, and there is thanksgiving. There is worship, and there is celebration. But there is something in the songs of the psalmists that is missing from our contemporary songs.

For example, where is the confusion of Psalm 13:2?

> *How long must I struggle with anguish in my soul,*
> *with sorrow in my heart every day?*

Or the misery of Psalm 32:3?

> *My body wasted away,*
> *and I groaned all day long.*

Where are the tears of Psalm 42:3?

> *Day and night I have only tears for food.*

Or the brokenness of Psalm 51:3?

> *For I recognize my rebellion;*
> *it haunts me day and night.*

Where is the desperation of Psalm 69:1-2?

> *Save me, O God,*
> *for the floodwaters are up to my neck.*
> *Deeper and deeper I sink into the mire;*
> *I can't find a foothold.*

Or the loneliness of Psalm 102:6-7?

> *I am like an owl in the desert,*
> *like a little owl in a far-off wilderness.*
> *I lie awake,*
> *lonely as a solitary bird on the roof.*

The emotions expressed in these verses are largely absent from the songs we sing on Sunday mornings.

Why?

Because we want songs that are uplifting. So we edit out the sadness, taking out the discordant notes, the chorus of questions, the melancholy tones. And this is the result. Our songs give the impression that there is no room in the church for our sadness, no room for our questions, our confusion, our despair. And if there is no room for those things, we can't help but wonder, *Is there any room for us?*

Prolonged suffering, regardless of whether it is physical or emotional, can edge us to the periphery of church life and sometimes usher us out the door altogether. We feel shunned, not by the scorn of our elders, but by the strum of upbeat stanzas in our corporate worship.

In our songbooks there are no lyrics with unanswered questions, no dissonant verses that are left dangling, no sorrow that is allowed its time to mourn. So church, which should be a warm, hospitable place where we can find rest for our souls, becomes an indifferent inn with no room.

So we stop going altogether.

Or we come late and leave early.

Or else we simply settle into the pews and keep our sadness to ourselves.

Here is the truth we are able to melt down from the verses quoted earlier. In the Psalms there is room for the bipolar swing of emotions that suffering evokes. Room for our questions, our doubts, our fears. There is even room for our anger. We come there with a sigh of relief and find a place where we can sit with others who share some of the same feelings. For those whose lives have been shattered by loss, there is no place in the Scriptures as hospitable as the Psalms.

The church should be such a place corporately, and we who are its members should be such a place individually. Here is the hope we should have when we go to church—not that there is no sorrow in the room but that there is no room where our sorrow is not welcome.

For if there is a stable for our sorrow, there is always the possibility of Christ being born in the midst of the darkest of our circumstances.

Coming as King.

Claiming his throne.

And establishing his Kingdom within us.

A Kingdom where the wolf in us and the lamb in us will at last be able to lie down together.

A PRAYER FOR HOSPITALITY

Dear Lord,

Help me to be a hospitable place for those who are suffering,
so that they may be able to lay down their burdens
and find rest for their weary souls.

Enlarge my heart so there will be room for their frustration,
their confusion, their anger.

Help me to show hospitality to the stranger with unbearable pain,
knowing that some, in doing so, have entertained angels.

Help me to make room in my heart for my own suffering,
a stable for my confusion,
a manger for my tears,
and swaddling clothes for the heavenly gift
that labors to be born there.

CHAPTER THREE

CLIMBING ALONE

Beside the rivers of Babylon, we sat and wept
as we thought of Jerusalem.
We put away our harps,
hanging them on the branches of poplar trees.
For our captors demanded a song from us.
Our tormentors insisted on a joyful hymn:
"Sing us one of those songs of Jerusalem!"
But how can we sing the songs of the Lord
while in a pagan land?

PSALM 137:1-4

ROPES are one of a climber's most essential pieces of equipment. Roped to a partner, a climber can stay the course if his eyes are blinded by the snow or his mind becomes disoriented from the altitude. A taut rope can keep a climber from slipping on scree or save him from plunging down a crevasse. It can stabilize his steps in high winds or save his life in an avalanche.

Many who have fallen to their deaths on Everest were climbers who didn't think they needed a rope . . . or a partner. They thought they could do it on their own—took pride in the fact that they could do it on their own. Sadly, many of those climbers never came back. Instead, their deaths have become cautionary tales for other climbers, and their bodies frozen monuments to their hubris.

This is the story of one such climber named George Frey.

Tenzing Norgay, in his autobiography titled *Tiger of the Snows*, writes about the experience of climbing Kang Peak in the Himalayas with Frey on a 1952 Swiss expedition:

> *At first the going was easy enough, following a long snow slope into which we could kick good steps, and not so steep that we needed a rope between us. But after a while the angle grew a bit sharper, and the snow harder, and I stopped and put on my steel-spiked crampons, so as to have a steadier footing. "Aren't you going to put yours on?" I called up to Frey, who was in the lead. "No, I don't*

need them," he answered. And we continued climbing. Once again there is the question of whether I should have done otherwise—such as arguing or urging more strongly. But Frey, as I have said, was an excellent climber. He had had much experience in the Alps, had certainly been in much more difficult places than where we were now, and seemed to be having no trouble. We continued smoothly and easily—he first, myself second, Ang Dawa third—still unroped and with perhaps fifteen feet between us; and looking around, I judged that we were at about 17,000 feet, with only another 2,000 to go to the top of Kang Peak.

Then Frey slipped. Just how or why, I could not tell. But one moment he was climbing steadily above me and in the next he was plunging down. At first it looked as if he were going to fall right on top of me and carry me along with him, but actually he was a little to one side, and as he came by I dug in and lunged and tried to hold him. It was hopeless, though; there was too much weight and momentum. His body struck my outstretched hand, there was a quick, sharp pain in one finger, and then he was past me—past Ang Dawa, below me—falling and tumbling down the mountainside until he came to rest on a flat place about a thousand feet below.

The parallels in the spiritual realm are frightening. In a moment, we can lose our footing. A moral misstep when our marriage feels shaky, and it can lead to an affair. An emotional misstep when we're going through depression, and it can lead to the loss of a job or the loss of a friendship. A spiritual misstep when we're suffering, and it can lead to our falling away from God, falling so hard and so far that it might lead to paralysis of some of the feelings we once had for spiritual things, even to the death of those feelings. This is why the rope is so essential. If we are not roped to other caring Christians, it could result in a catastrophic fall like the one Frey experienced.

▲ ▲ ▲

The early British expeditions to scale Mount Everest followed a route by the North Ridge. In the spring of 1924, Howard Somervell and

Edward Norton climbed the North Face. Suffering physical problems during the ascent, Somervell unroped himself from Norton, who continued climbing to an altitude of 28,126 feet before turning back to help his partner. Later Norton wrote how treacherous the North Face was:

> The whole face of the mountain was composed of slabs like the tiles
> on a roof, and all sloped at much the same angle as the tiles. . . . It
> was not exactly difficult going, but it was a dangerous place for a
> single unroped climber, as one slip would have sent me in all
> probability to the bottom of the mountain.

After C. S. Lewis became a Christian, he enjoyed a scenic view of the peaks of faith from the windows of his study at an ivy-covered English university. Then tragedy stuck, and he found himself on the North Face of God.

In *A Grief Observed*, Lewis's journal of his spiritual climb after the death of his wife, Joy, to cancer, he is honest and forthright about his emotions and how precarious the footing had become for him. Expressing emotion openly was always something Lewis felt uncomfortable doing, even embarrassed doing, but the journal gave him a safe place. Lewis's stepson, Douglas Gresham, tells of a rare occasion when his stepfather did display his emotion.

When the fourteen-year-old Gresham came to The Kilns upon hearing the news of his mother's death, he opened the front door and saw Lewis, whom the boy knew as Jack, standing by the fireplace. He was shocked by Lewis's appearance. Gresham describes the encounter in his book *Lenten Lands*, about his childhood with his mother, Joy Davidman, and C. S. Lewis:

> I had last seen him merely ten days or so previously, but since that
> time he had aged twenty years or more. His eyes held the look of a
> soul in Hell. My brittle shell smashed, and I broke. "Oh, Jack," I
> burst out, and then the tears came. Jack rushed across the room and
> put his arm around me. I held on to him, as we both wept. That was
> the only occasion of which any physical demonstration of our love for

*each other ever occurred. "Jack," I finally said, "What are we going
to do?" He looked at me, his compassion for me showing through his
own grief. "Just carry on somehow, I suppose, Doug."*

Somehow, Jack and Doug did carry on. But Lewis was never the
same. Not only had he lost Joy, but he had lost joy for everything.
Aside from that single outward show of emotion, he carried his grief
inside him, silently and privately. To vent his feelings, he jotted
them down in the pages of a children's composition book he had at
home. Day after day he returned to those pages, finally filling three
of those books and spilling over to a fourth. The feelings he expressed are raw. The doubts are real. The prose is random, without
thought to structure or transitions or even coherence.

The following entry in Lewis's journal captures not only his disillusionment but also his anger: "What chokes every prayer and every
hope is the memory of all the prayers [we] offered and all the false
hopes we had. Not hopes raised merely by our own wishful thinking;
hopes encouraged, even forced upon us, by false diagnoses, by
X-ray photographs, by strange remissions, by one temporary recov-
ery that might have ranked as a miracle. Step by step we were 'led up
the garden path.' Time after time, when He seemed most gracious
He was already preparing the next torture."

The next torture?

Sounds a little melodramatic, doesn't it?

Not to Jeremiah, the Old Testament prophet who saw his whole
world go up in smoke during the destruction of Jerusalem. Listen to
the wail in his words:

> *"He has walled me in, and I cannot escape.*
> *He has bound me in heavy chains.*
> *And though I cry and shout,*
> *he has shut out my prayers.*
> *He has blocked my way with a high stone wall;*
> *he has made my road crooked.*
> *He has hidden like a bear or a lion,*
> *waiting to attack me.*

He has dragged me off the path and torn me in pieces,
leaving me helpless and devastated.
He has drawn his bow
and made me the target for his arrows." (Lamentations 3:7-12)

Sounds a lot like torture to me. So do David's words in Psalm
38:2: "Your arrows have struck deep, and your blows are crushing
me."

For Lewis, the days, weeks, and months after his wife's death were
sheer torture. Douglas Gresham observed the toll it took on his
stepfather:

> *It has been said that Jack's years at Cambridge after Mother's death*
> *were happy. That is not true. Jack, when in company with his friends*
> *and colleagues, was (after a while) again the jovial, witty intellectual*
> *they had known for years, but only Warnie [Lewis's brother] and I*
> *knew the effort that cost him, and Warnie knew less than I, for Jack*
> *was careful with Warnie; I was more invisible. Jack's colleagues and*
> *friends never saw him as he turned from waving a cheery good-bye at*
> *the door of The Kilns and casting some pearls of parting witticism to a*
> *departing guest; they never watched him suddenly slump, his whole*
> *body shrinking like a slowly deflating balloon, his face losing the light*
> *of laughter and becoming grey, until he became once more a tired,*
> *sick and grieving man, old beyond his years.*

After Joy's death, Lewis's life deteriorated—physically, emotionally,
spiritually, and socially. Creatively, he mainly tied up the loose ends
of the projects he had been working on before her death, polishing
a final draft of essays, correcting some chronological errors in The
Chronicles of Narnia, and making dwindling finishes to *Letters to
Malcolm* and *Letters to an American Lady*, which were collections of his
correspondence.

Partly due to his natural British reserve and partly because he was
a very private person, Lewis grieved alone. He concealed his true
feelings even from his closest friends, and this was partly due to the
fact that none of them, with the exception of Austin Farrer, came to

his wife's funeral. He never asked why, and they never told him, but their absence hurt him deeply, and he felt betrayed.

You would think he would have opened up to his brother. After all, they lived in the same house together. But even his brother was unaware of the heaviness of his grief, as his stepson notes:

> *Even Warnie did not know, but boys are sometimes hard to see, and many times I watched Jack, unseen by him, as he walked, his mind clear, through the pain of his own Gethsemane. On his way to Warnie's study, tray in hand, he would stop, take a deep breath, pull back his shoulders, raise his head and bring his facial expression under control, then, bold and cheerful of countenance, he would step into the study with a glad cry of "Tea, brother."*

Lewis worked through his anger and his confusion and made his peace with God. But he was never the same. He seemed to sit on a ledge of grief, breathing in the thin air and waiting for the end of his life, which he hoped would be soon. Joy died in July 1960. Lewis died on November 22, 1963, a week shy of his sixty-fifth birthday.

I felt sad when I learned how inward one of my favorite authors had become, how isolated he was from the very relationships that had once been such a source of happiness. A good friend would have made a difference, I think. If a friend would have pursued him, pushed through his reserve and tied a rope of encouragement and hope around his waist, years of his life could have been saved.

Although C. S. Lewis was a man of many friends, intimacy with those friends was difficult for him. He could never endure the embrace of a friend, something he would later write about, calling it a weakness in his character: "An unmanly weakness by the way; Aeneas, Beowulf, Roland, Launcelot, Johnson, and Nelson knew nothing of it."

There are things in life we must do alone, but walking through the valley of the shadow of death is not one of them. When we mourn the loss of someone we love, it helps to mourn in community with others who feel the pain of our loss.

When the Jews were driven into exile by the Babylonians, they mourned the loss of the city they loved, the land they loved, the way of life they loved, as well as many of their loved ones who had been killed resisting capture. They mourned together as a community and not in isolation. Wearied from the trudging march forced by their captors, they sat down together beside the rivers of Babylon, and together they wept.

Don McLean, the singer who sang the popular songs "American Pie" and "Vincent," also sang the less-popular "Babylon," whose lyrics come from Psalm 137. Unlike his other songs, McLean doesn't sing this one alone. He invites the audience to join in. Somehow that seems appropriate because it begs for the accompaniment of other hearts and voices.

There are songs that were never meant to be sung alone, valleys that were never meant to be walked alone.

Grief is one of those valleys.

And weeping is one of those songs.

When I was writing this book, I went to a funeral for a little girl who had been killed in a car wreck. Before the service started, people in the pews were sniffling back tears, heads bowed, wiping the sadness from their eyes. The mother of the girl was sobbing so hard she could hardly stand as she walked in. She was seated in the front row, along with the rest of her family, when the singing started. All the songs were praise songs, positive and upbeat. After a couple of songs, everyone had stopped crying—except the mother. Her tears were unabated.

When the service was over, she was ushered away, still sobbing. I wonder, did the praise and worship songs help that despondent mother? Or did they only make her feel more lonely, more isolated from the rest of us?

Personally, I wanted to cry, *needed* to cry—for the little girl, certainly, but also for her family. That morning the mother needed music that fit her brokenness. And she found none. Maybe silence is the best music for such a time—silence and the sound of other people weeping.

Together.

A PRAYER FOR STRENGTH

Dear Lord,

Sometimes I feel like a stranger in a foreign land,
displaced and dispirited.

The grief I carry is so heavy, and I have carried it so long
that sometimes I just want to sit down and have a good cry.

I feel like hanging it all up—
the way the Jews hung up their harps
on the branches of those poplar trees.

I am tormented by all the joyful songs I am expected to sing.

But how can I sing those songs while I am where I am,
in this land that is so foreign,
with these feelings that are so foreign?

Give me the lyrics I need, Lord, and the tune to go with them.

Give me the strength to sing the songs I need to sing,
along with the voices of others to sing with me.

For I can't do this as a solo.

I just can't.

Connect me to other believers, Lord.

Rope me to kindred spirits with caring hearts
so that whatever valleys we must pass through,
—however dark, however deep—
we will pass through them together.

camp iii

▲

Altitude: 20,200 Feet

A raging fever burns within me,
and my health is broken.
I am exhausted and completely crushed.
My groans come from an
anguished heart.

You know what I long for, Lord;
you hear my every sigh.
My heart beats wildly, my strength fails,
and I am going blind.
My loved ones and friends stay away,
fearing my disease.
Even my own family stands at a distance.
PSALM 38:7-11

Camp III marks the end of the Khumbu Icefall and the beginning of our ascent up the Western Cwm (a Welsh word, pronounced *koom*, which means "a valley formed by a glacier"). This glacial valley winds upward through the mountains and is layered with swells of unstable snow. Ladders are necessary to bridge the many crevasses. And ropes are essential because the footing is so precarious.

Camp III lies at 20,200 feet, and anyone who has reached that altitude feels the effects. Heart rate increases, strength decreases, and a climber's eyes sometimes experience temporary blindness due to oxygen deprivation in the brain's visual cortex.

In Psalm 38:10, something similar seems to be happening to David:

My heart beats wildly, my strength fails,
and I am going blind.

Things are not going well with him. He's bent over and racked with pain (v. 6), his body is inflamed with fever (v. 7), and he's utterly exhausted (v. 8). If ever he needed someone roped to him to pull him to safety, it is now. Yet tragically, his friends and loved ones stay away, and his family stands at a distance (v. 11).

The ties that bind us together can sometimes be constricting, chafing us with a sudden twist of the rope. But those same ties can also belay us to safety. Family, friends, loved ones—we need them. That was what David needed, and what we all have needed at one time or another. Solomon said as much when he wrote, "Two people are better off than one, for they can help each other succeed. If one person falls, the other can reach out and help. But someone who falls alone is in real trouble. Likewise, two people lying close together can keep each other warm. But how can one be warm alone? A person standing alone can be attacked and defeated, but two can stand back-to-back and conquer" (Ecclesiastes 4:9-12).

The Scriptures are replete with examples. Moses had Aaron. David had Jonathan. Paul had Barnabas and later Silas. "Three are even better," contends Solomon, "for a triple-braided cord is not easily broken" (v. 12). Jesus understood the wisdom of Solomon's advice. When crossing the Kidron Valley to Gethsemane, he "roped" himself to his three closest friends—Peter, James, and John.

Two are better than one when climbing Mount Everest. Three are even better. A full team of climbing partners is better still. Yes, the mountain has been climbed alone. Reinhold Messner, the legendary Italian climber, was the first to do it in 1980.

Others came after him.

Extremely skilled climbers, all of them.

And extremely lucky.

I have done my share of climbing alone, both literally and figuratively. The mountains I have traipsed up are a third the height of Everest, with gentle slopes and well-marked trails, and there was never any danger. But I have had my own times when God has seemed more like the North Face of Everest than a well-hiked trail, times when I was determined to scale whatever slope I needed to, no matter how steep or how slippery, in order to find some answers. Many of those times I traveled alone. I wonder now, as I look back on those times, why. Why didn't I ask someone to come with me? Why didn't I at least ask for directions?

Was I just an ambitious climber who felt he needed to make the climb alone in order to get his name in the record books? Was I a purist who felt that climbing with a partner and using bottled oxygen were somehow taking unfair advantage? Was I just too proud to ask for help? Or too naive to think I needed it?

I can't speak for others who have made the climb. But for me, it was none of those things. I think the reason I have so seldom asked for help is that I didn't think anyone would really care that much to make the climb with me. Not that I didn't have caring friends. I did. And a caring wife too.

I think I felt I wasn't all that worth caring about. And maybe that is one of the gifts we receive along the way. Someone asks to come along with us, to be roped to us for the climb. Or several someones. It's humbling to realize that it's not the climb they are interested in—it's us, you and me. They take enormous risks to make sure we make it down alive. Why? Because they love us. Because they love us, and they think we're worth the effort.

And that should warm each of us to the bone, regardless of how far we are from our faith or how frostbitten our feelings.

A PRAYER FOR MY FRIENDS

Dear Lord,

Your Son told his disciples,

"I no longer call you servants but friends."

And it is true what the hymn says,

"What a friend we have in Jesus."

But it is also true that you have given us flesh–and–blood friends
*   to be his hands and his feet,*
*   his eyes and his ears,*
*   his heart and his voice.*

Thank you for those you have recruited as my climbing partners,
*   to hack steps in the ice,*
*   to keep an eye on the weather,*
*   to encourage me when I tire,*
*   to steady me when I stumble,*
*   to catch me when I fall.*

Never let me think I can make it without them, Lord.

Thank you that the risks they have taken are not for the summit but for me.

Help me to realize that each step is the beginning of a fall
*   and that without those very special friends,*
*   the fall could be fatal.*

CHAPTER FOUR

LOOKING BEYOND
THE CLOUDS

Do not be afraid . . .
For he will order his angels
to protect you wherever you go.
They will hold you up with their hands
so you won't even hurt your foot
on a stone.
PSALM 91:5, 11-12

THE HIMALAYAS are often veiled with clouds, but now and then there is a break in the weather, lifting that veil, and the vast expanse of the range is revealed. The same is true of the experiences that make up our lives. Most of the time, all we see is the physical world. But now and then there is a parting of the clouds, and we are given a glimpse of the spiritual world and how it affects us.

Consider the glimpse we receive, for example, when Jesus reveals the role that Satan played in Peter's denial (Luke 22:31). Or the glimpse when Jesus revealed the role Satan played in Judas's betrayal (John 13:27). How much of the adversity in our lives, I wonder, happens because Satan and his forces are working behind the scenes?

More than we know, I'm certain.

Maybe more than we could ever imagine.

Sometimes the work of the enemy is so relentless that we can hardly believe it. Such has been the case in the life of a friend of mine I'll call Jim.

Jim grew up in a small East Texas town with an alcoholic father, a domineering mother, and a sadistic older brother. Jim's earliest memories are memories of abuse. Some at home. Some in the neighborhood. And some at school.

The abuse started at home with his older brother. As Jim was learning to walk, his brother would sometimes throw sofa pillows at his feet, knocking him down and causing him to hit his head on the tile floor. Thinking it all great sport, his brother laughed as little Jim cried and struggled to get up and try again. Later, on at least one occasion, his brother pummeled Jim's head against the closet door until he was so dizzy and disoriented that he fell to the floor. And as Jim got up and staggered away, his brother just laughed. Outside, his brother would throw hard green tomatoes from the family garden, hitting Jim in the head so hard it knocked him down. Jim became the never-ending target of his brother's ridicule and cruelty, from pulling down Jim's pants and snickering to calling him names such as "Googles" and "Four-eyed Bat" when he began wearing glasses.

The Greek philosopher Bion once said, "Though boys throw stones at frogs in sport, the frogs do not die in sport, but in earnest." And die Jim did. One demeaning remark at a time. One devious prank at a time. One devilish laugh at a time. Each incident of abuse sent a stone grazing across his tender, young heart. Those wounds live with him to this day. He is haunted by the images of his past, humiliated by the echoes of his brother's voice reminding him how inferior he was, how unloved he was, and how unwanted.

That voice was given credence by an absence of affection from Jim's father and the vacillating affections of his mother. His father's heavy drinking and smoking made him old beyond his years. He worked long hours, often away from home, and when he *was* home, he was tired, sick, and emotionally inaccessible. His smoking finally took its toll, and after battling cancer for two years, he died when Jim was ten. Although his father had been inaccessible, at least he was predictably so. On the other hand, nothing about Jim's mother was predictable. She was an emotional minefield covered with wildflowers. Everything would look lovely and serene on the surface, until Jim would make one wrong step, and then she would blow up in his face. From day to day he would never know what her mood would be.

The abuse from the neighborhood came from an older boy. It started when Jim was four. The older boy talked him into getting naked and then fondled him. Over the years he engaged Jim in various sex acts. The abuse didn't stop until years later when the older boy moved away.

This was Jim's secret shame, making him feel like an abused

animal—wet, shivering, and scared. He felt safer in the shadows, but the shadows held a terror of their own. In the shadows of his secret, he felt beyond the reach of human understanding, let alone compassion. He felt dirty inside. As he grew older, the shadows lengthened—so much so that he felt beyond the reach of healthy male friendships and beyond the reach of romance with females.

Worst of all, he felt beyond the reach of God.

At school the abuse came at the hands of other players on his baseball team, the boys in his gym class, his coaches, and one of his teachers. His coaches and teammates ridiculed his playing ability and blamed him for losing one of their games. Their taunting was so relentless that he quit playing sports altogether.

In gym class, the other boys made fun of him because he was physically underdeveloped for his age. But where do you go to quit gym? Where do you go to hide from the bullies in the locker room? How do you stop the comments from spilling over into the hallways, the cafeteria, the classroom? And do you dare go to the restroom? No teacher would protect him in the restroom, no one would shield him from the ogling stares, the finger-pointing, the wisecracks, the pushing and shoving.

The other abuse at school came from his sixth-grade science teacher, an emotionally unstable woman who routinely chose one child each school year to intimidate and humiliate. Wouldn't you know it? She picked Jim. Once, she accused him in class of calling her on the telephone and cussing her out, going on to say that his parents had always been ashamed of him. Of course, he hadn't called her, but how can an eleven-year-old boy defend himself from the intimidation of such an authority figure? All Jim could do was sit at his desk, completely humiliated, and sob uncontrollably. Although the teacher was reprimanded for her actions, the damage had already been done. And throughout the remainder of the year, she persisted in accusing him of imaginary infractions and correcting him, both in the classroom and on the playground.

Jim coped by applying himself diligently to his studies. In high school, he received some of the highest honors a student could attain—student council president, Who's Who, senior editor of the yearbook, and numerous leadership awards. But in spite of the accolades, he was lonely.

When he graduated, he went to college, but there he was even more isolated, more lonely. Desperately insecure, he found himself caught in a swirling vortex of depression. He cried a lot and became increasingly aware of his own sinfulness. With no one to turn to, he considered suicide.

Fortunately, through contact with a campus ministry, Jim became a Christian.

You might think that coming to Christ would have ended his torment, ended his shame, ended his loneliness. But it didn't. In fact, his internal conflicts intensified. Anytime he tried to memorize Scripture or meditate on God, anytime he tried to pray or worship, he was assaulted by a rush of blasphemous thoughts and images. Even when he looked at a beautiful sunset or sat down to a sumptuous meal, evil thoughts came rushing in.

"No matter how much I studied the Scriptures," he said, "and no matter how hard I prayed, my thoughts grew worse. I came to dread time alone with God; the pursuit of the One I needed most resulted in my greater sense of alienation and shame."

Jim kept many of these things to himself, hoping that if he read the right books, listened to the right preachers, and attended the right seminars, he would find the key to unlock the cell that was so mercilessly holding him captive. Although the books, tapes, and seminars all had keys to freedom of some kind or another, none of those keys worked for Jim. His failure to find release only added to his shame and loneliness, making him feel like an incurable leper, forever banished to a colony outside the gated community of victorious Christians. The few people he turned to for help during that time merely made matters worse.

From what I have written about Jim, you might picture him as a homeless man, living among a tenement of cardboard boxes in some back alley reeking of cheap wine and rotting garbage. You might picture him as friendless and filled with bitterness. You might picture him reclusive and incapable of holding down a job.

He is, in fact, a very successful businessman. He is an enthralling storyteller with a great sense of humor and really enjoyable to be around. He has good friends, and I am proud to be counted among them. He is talented and intelligent, a good listener and sensitive to other people's pain. He is gracious and polite and kind. He loves God and longs for all the right things. He wants to be married, have children, the white-picket-fenced home, everything. He wants what we all want, what so many of us have found so effortlessly in abundance.

More than anything, though, he wants release from the guilt, the shame, the loneliness—release from the horrible thoughts and tormenting images. But after years of praying and years of crying, he feels his prayers have fallen on deaf ears. And of all the painful things Jim has experienced in life, that is the most difficult to bear. As C. S. Lewis said, "We can bear to be refused but not to be ignored."

Although Jim is a grown man, something of the little boy that was hurt so badly so many years ago lives in him to this day. Jim wonders about that boy, wonders if there was anything he could have done back then to protect him and if there is anything he can do now to understand him, to befriend him, to heal him.

He wonders too how Jesus feels about that boy. The country-western group Alabama has a song with the refrain "The closest thing to heaven is a child." The words are a paraphrase of Jesus' teaching in Matthew 18, and they express, I think, how Jesus feels about children and how he feels about the child who still lives in you, in me, in all of us.

At the beginning of Matthew 18, Jesus' disciples come to him asking which of them was greatest in the Kingdom of Heaven. Instead of pointing to one of them, he points to a small child, calls him over, and puts him in the center of his disciples. "I tell you the truth," Jesus tells them, "unless you turn from your sins and become like little children, you will never get into the Kingdom of Heaven. So anyone who becomes as humble as this little child is the greatest in the Kingdom of Heaven" (vv. 3-4).

While Jesus walked this earth, his feelings for children were no mystery. He gathered them in his arms, blessed them, healed them, delivered them from demonic oppression, and used them to reveal his Father's heart.

"It is not my heavenly Father's will," Jesus says, "that even one of these little ones should perish" (v. 14). He goes so far as to say, "But if you cause one of these little ones who trusts in me to fall into sin, it would be better for you to have a large millstone tied around your neck and be drowned in the depths of the sea. What sorrow awaits the world, because it tempts people to sin. Temptations are inevitable, but what sorrow awaits the person who does the tempting" (vv. 6-7).

How dear are children to God? So dear that he has vowed to bring judgment on anyone who harms them or does anything that causes them to lose faith. God's judgment serves as a deterrent, but to further protect children, he has assigned angels to watch over them. "Beware that you don't look down on any of these little ones," Jesus warns. "For I tell you that in heaven their angels are always in the presence of my heavenly Father" (v. 10).

It was a Jewish belief that nations (such as Persia, Greece, and Israel) had spirit beings watching over them (Daniel 10:13, 20-21). The early Christians held a similar belief with regard to specific local churches (such as those in Ephesus, Sardis, and Laodicea; see Revelation 2:1; 3:1, 14). Jesus describes the angels that watch over children as the ones who are "always in the presence of my heavenly Father" (Matthew 18:10). This rank of angels would be parallel to the highest court officials who have continual access to a king.

When you put these verses together, the teaching of Christ is clear: Protecting children is one of God's highest priorities.

What isn't so clear is this: If children are so dear to God and if he is so determined to protect them, why do terrible things sometimes happen to them?

To answer that question, we have to look at the world as it really is, not as we would like it to be. We must turn our heads away from the Disney Channel to the Discovery Channel, where a common scene from the physical world gives us a glimpse into the realities of the spiritual world.

You remember the programs, I'm sure. The ones with the lion prowling in the tall grass, its tawny coat blending with the surroundings. What is the lion's strategy? Does it go charging into the middle of a herd of adult zebras? No. It stalks the herd, crouching, watching, waiting. And what is it waiting for? A young zebra to stray from the herd. Then, at an opportune moment, the lion springs from the grass, runs the zebra down, tears it to pieces, and devours it.

When seeing such brutality, one can't help but think that something has gone terribly wrong with nature. The truth is, it has. Nature reflects the fallenness of the world. What we see in the natural realm is a shadow of what takes place in the spiritual realm. Thus, when Peter describes the devil, he pictures him as a roaring lion that prowls the earth, looking for some victim to devour (1 Peter 5:8).

Is it any wonder he preys so persistently on children?

And if children are his prey, where are their angels when the devil is on the prowl?

Despite how safe and secure our neighborhoods may seem on the surface, we live in a war-torn world where the forces of good and evil are engaged in the most intense of battles. Here and there in the Scriptures, the veil is lifted, and we are shown something of the battles being fought over us, both the spiritual battles (Job 1) and the physical battles (2 Kings 6:16-17). Another passage where the veil is lifted is in Daniel 10–11.

While serving under the reign of a Persian king, Daniel received a vision from God, after which he prayed and fasted for three weeks. At the end of those three weeks, an angel came to visit Daniel. When Daniel looked up, he "saw a man dressed in linen clothing, with a belt of pure gold around his waist. His body looked like a precious gem. His face flashed like lightning, and his eyes flamed like torches. His arms and feet shone like polished bronze, and his voice roared like a vast multitude of people" (Daniel 10:5-6). Terrified, Daniel fell to the ground. The angel then took him by the hand and spoke to him: "Daniel, you are very precious to God, so listen carefully to what I have to say to you. Stand up, for I have been sent to you" (v. 11).

When Daniel rose, trembling, to his feet, the angel said:

> *"Don't be afraid, Daniel. Since the first day you began to pray for*
> *understanding and to humble yourself before your God, your request*

*has been heard in heaven. I have come in answer to your prayer.
But for twenty-one days the spirit prince of the kingdom of Persia
blocked my way. Then Michael, one of the archangels, came to help
me, and I left him there with the spirit prince of the kingdom of
Persia" (vv. 12-13).*

Before the angel left, he lifted the veil a little higher:

*"Soon I must return to fight against the spirit prince of the kingdom
of Persia, and after that the spirit prince of the kingdom of Greece
will come. . . . (No one helps me against these spirit princes except
Michael, your spirit prince. I have been standing beside Michael to
support and strengthen him since the first year of the reign of Darius
the Mede.)" (10:20-21—11:1)*

What's comforting about this incident is that Daniel's prayer was
heard, and help was dispatched immediately. What's unsettling is
that for twenty-one days the will of heaven was thwarted because of
opposition in the spirit realm.

Daniel 10—11 is not a Hallmark greeting card; it's a soldier's account from the front lines. And the angel giving the account isn't
soft-spoken and endearing; he's fierce and terrifying.

How formidable must the opposition be to have delayed such a
warrior?

How fierce the combat to have lasted so long?

Thinking about that combat raises some questions about the battles that have been fought over you and me. How many battles, I
wonder, were fought over us as children? And how many are still
being fought over us as adults?

How fierce are the assaults—and how valiant the defense? How
long did they rage? At what cost were the victories achieved? At what
cost the defeats? And how many attacks never reached us because
some angel fought his heart out, taking the blows that were meant
for us?

Which brings me back to Jim.

Where was *his* angel when he needed him?

Where was *ours*?

I can't say for sure, but my guess is he was fighting his heart out—and is fighting it out still.

PRAYING OUR QUESTIONS

Dear Lord,

I don't understand why bad things happen to good people,
*   especially when those people are children.*

Where were your angels when I was one of those children?

That child still lives in me . . . still wonders . . . still cries.

Lift a veil on my past, Lord,
*   help me to see something of the spiritual battle*
*   that was fought over me.*

Help me to understand the defeats in those battles
*   and the delays to my prayers.*

Thank you for the angel whose assignment was me.

Does he have a name, I wonder, as Daniel's angel did?

Thank you for sending him to watch over me.

Thank you for thinking I was worth watching over,
*   worth coming for, worth fighting for.*

I pray that the angel who watched over me as a child
*   could see that child now*
*   and be proud to have watched over me so vigilantly*
*   and to have fought for me so valiantly.*

Keep watching over me, Lord.

And keep fighting.

camp iv

▲

Altitude: 21,200 feet

The LORD is king! Let the earth rejoice!
Let the farthest coastlands be glad.
Dark clouds surround him.
Righteousness and justice are
the foundation of his throne.
PSALM 97:1-2

In 1988 Stephen Venables, along with three climbing partners, attempted to reach the summit of Mount Everest by the most challenging route: the Kangshung Face, a sheer wall of snow, some eleven-thousand-feet high. George Mallory, one of the first two Westerners to see the Kangshung Face, had taken one look and dismissed it as impossible to climb.

Even to Venables's contemporaries, the climb seemed foolhardy. The team was too small. The angle, too steep. The outcroppings, too great. And avalanches, too common.

Of the four in the team, only Venables made it to the top. In his account of the climb, *Everest: Alone at the Summit,* he writes about his view from the peak: "When I could find the strength to stand up again I looked down the West Ridge, which disappeared into swirling clouds. There was no sign of the British Services Expedition. Then I turned to the right, where the Northeast Ridge—the 'Mallory Route'—also dropped away in the clouds. I could not see the Rongbuk Glacier, nor the Kama valley, and to the south there were yet more clouds, completely hiding Lhotse from view."

In spite of the fact that he was on the summit, clouds obscured his view. The same can happen in the spiritual realm. Even though we may reach a summit of understanding, everything may still not be clear. The psalmist hints at this when he says:

The LORD is king! Let the earth rejoice!
Let the farthest coastlands be glad.
Dark clouds surround him.
Righteousness and justice are
the foundation of his throne.
PSALM 97:1-2

The Lord is King, but for all the clouds, we can't see the far reaches of his rule. The foundations of his throne are righteousness and justice, but darkness obscures our understanding of how a sovereign God could tolerate all the wickedness and injustice that run rampant through the earth.

We may never reach a summit of understanding where suddenly everything is clear. For some cliffs are unscalable; some crevasses unbridgeable. And we may find ourselves stranded beneath an overhang, unable to climb any higher. But even if we do reach the summit, only patches of the surrounding panorama may be visible because of the clouds.

If we are someday granted the grace to sit on that summit—and it's a clear day—I think we will feel humbled by what we see. And honored. Honored to be given a glimpse of the grand sweep of God's story. Humbled to know that we have played a part in the story, however small a part and for however brief a time.

Joseph came to such a summit of understanding when the very brothers who had betrayed him came to him years later for help. "Do not be afraid," he told them, "for am I in God's place? As for you, you meant evil against me, but God meant it for good in order to bring about this present result, to preserve many people alive" (Genesis 50:19-20, NASB).

Moses was also given a summit of understanding on top of Mount Nebo. There the Lord showed him the full extent of the land he had promised the nation. "Then the Lord said to Moses, 'This is the land I promised on oath to Abraham, Isaac, and Jacob when I said, "I will give it to your descendants." I have now allowed you see it with your own eyes, but you will not enter the land'" (Deuteronomy 34:4).

The apostle Paul was given perhaps the greatest glimpse of God's purposes when he was taken to heaven (2 Corinthians 12:1-4), seeing things there that human eyes had never before seen, hearing things that human ears had never before heard.

There will come a time when each and every one of us will look on our lives from the vantage point of eternity and see that our entire lifetime was just a moment to God, a mere breath. So was our suffering. Then we will look on the rewards that have been stored up for us, rewards for our faithfulness as stewards of the heavy talents of suffering that were entrusted to us. And we will be startled to see that the exchange rate of heaven is not measured out to us pound for pound because the thumb of a generous God is on those scales, weighting them in our favor.

"That is why we never give up, . . ." the apostle Paul says. "For our present troubles are small and won't last very long. Yet they produce for us a glory that vastly outweighs them and will last forever! So we don't look at the troubles we can see now; rather, we fix our gaze on things that cannot be seen. For the things we see now will soon be gone, but the things we cannot see will last forever" (2 Corinthians 4:16-18).

Though clouds may have obscured that reality from us, along with other realities, on a clear day on the summit we see not only the lay of the land but also the forces of evil roaming that land. Their boots in the stirrups of their horses. Their swords drawn. Their spears raised. We are the battlefield over which their war is waged. Our hearts, our souls, our very lives are the territory over which the hoofbeats of their horses thunder, kicking up dust as swords clash and the sound of steel against steel rings out.

But though our enemies are legion, the battle is still the Lord's. And though the fighting may be fierce, the victory is assured. Here is David's view from the summit of divine understanding in Psalm 3:

> *O LORD, I have so many enemies;*
> *so many are against me.*
> *So many are saying,*
> *"God will never rescue him!"*
> Interlude

But you, O LORD, are a shield around me;
you are my glory, the one who holds my head high.
I cried out to the LORD,
and he answered me from his holy mountain.
Interlude

I lay down and slept,
yet I woke up in safety,
for the LORD was watching over me.
I am not afraid of ten thousand enemies
who surround me on every side.

Arise, O LORD!

Rescue me, my God!
Slap all my enemies in the face!
Shatter the teeth of the wicked!
Victory comes from you, O LORD.
May you bless your people.

"A cloud of witnesses," we are told (Hebrews 12:1, NASB), views the battle we are engaged in, where they root for us, craning their necks to see how we fare. For the story of our lives is not just for us and those around us. It is for them as well. And maybe, just maybe, some of the understanding they get about their own stories comes from the playing out of ours.

Beyond the clouds others are watching too. The eyes of angelic beings, both good and evil, are also fixed on the battle. Why? Perhaps our stories, especially the stories of our suffering, are what God uses to silence the accusations of Satan. And perhaps it is our bravery in battle that he uses to stir the courage of angels. If we have entertained angels without knowing it, as the writer to the Hebrews asserts, maybe we have encouraged angels without knowing it.

Who knows how much they have needed the encouragement? The battle must take its toll on them as well. Certainly the swords they wield grow heavy in their hands. Certainly they lose heart too.

And they, like us, need the encouragement of other people's stories.

As remarkable as it may seem to you, some of those stories are yours.

And as remarkable as it seems to me, some of them are mine.

A PRAYER FOR VISION

Dear Lord,

Keep me from giving up,
for you know how tired I sometimes get,
and how discouraged.

Encourage me with a new perspective on my circumstances.

I pray, along with Paul, that you will help me to see
that my present troubles are so short-lived when compared to eternity;
so small when compared to the glory being produced in me.

Keep my eyes there, Lord, on the future that awaits me
instead of on the troubles that surround me.

Clouds are everywhere, at every altitude,
and it's so easy to lose my bearings.

I don't need to see everything, Lord,
but I do need to see something.

In your mercy, would you show me something? Please.

Show me something from the Scriptures,
something from the stories of others,
anything to strengthen me for the next step.

CHAPTER FIVE

FINDING A CAPABLE CLIMBING TEAM

He reached down from heaven and rescued me;
he drew me out of deep waters.
He rescued me from my powerful enemies,
from those who hated me and were too strong for me.
They attacked me at a moment when I was in distress,
but the LORD supported me.
He led me to a place of safety;
he rescued me because he delights in me.

PSALM 18:16-19

I N HIS BOOK *Summit Strategies: Secrets to Mastering the Everest in Your Life,* Gary Scott writes, "When your life is at stake, choosing your partners wisely is one of the most important preparations you can make."

Scott illustrates this truth with the story of a close friend named Trevor Pilling, a skilled and committed climber. The last time Gary saw Trevor was in a bar in Kathmandu at the end of a climbing expedition. When asked how the expedition had gone, Trevor sighed, pausing a long time before telling his story.

"It was a tragedy," he said, the color draining from his face as he spoke.

"What happened?" Gary asked.

"Phil didn't make it," he said.

Phil had been Trevor's climbing partner. He went on to explain: "Phil and I accepted a far-too-tempting last-minute invitation from two Welsh climbers, Mark and Steve, who had permission to climb a new route on Annapurna South [a 24,000-foot peak in central Nepal]. It wasn't until we reached our base camp that it became clear they weren't sufficiently experienced and needed us to give them any chance of success."

The group worked in teams of two. Mark and Steve established a third camp at 20,000 feet, then returned to the next lower camp to rest and recuperate. Trevor and Phil took off the next day, hoping to establish a fourth camp within fifteen hundred feet of the summit. They left at the first light of dawn. By midmorning, the sky had clotted, dark and foreboding. By noon, the blizzard hit.

With no place to shelter them from the galing winds, Trevor and Phil crawled into a shallow crevasse in the ice. Miraculously, they survived the night. The next morning Trevor noticed that Phil seemed distant and quiet.

Fighting the elements, Trevor found a place where he could dig a small cave in the snow. Digging took most of the morning. When he finished, he climbed back to where Phil was, and he was shocked at what he saw. Phil was lying outside his sleeping bag in a pool of vomit, mumbling to himself. His eyes were fixed and vacant.

Trevor pulled Phil into the cave and changed his clothes. He put him into his sleeping bag, but that was all he could do for him. Phil had lost his strength. He wouldn't eat, wouldn't drink. For the next two days, as they were pinned down by the storm, Phil drifted in and out of consciousness. When Trevor finally got his radio working, he called Mark and Steve at base camp, and they assured him they would help as soon as the storm cleared.

On the third morning the storm subsided. Trevor tried to get Phil moving, but Phil could hardly stand, let alone walk. Trevor knew that his friend would not be able to climb down the four-thousand-foot ice face. He radioed down to Dawa, their Sherpa cook, to ask when Mark and Steve had left. But it wasn't Dawa who answered; it was Steve.

"I yelled into the radio," Trevor said, "demanding to know why they hadn't left yet. In a very slow and rehearsed tone, Steve told me they weren't coming, that it was too dangerous. I tried to explain that the ridge we were on was too steep to be avalanche prone, but they didn't want to listen. I pleaded with them that they had to risk it. We would die if they didn't come and help me and Phil down."

Nothing Trevor said could change their minds. Although his own strength was dwindling and he was suffering from a severe, high-altitude headache, Trevor stayed with Phil another night, hoping against hope that help might come. When it didn't, he was faced with a fateful decision. "First thing the next morning I looked down the face, but there was no sign of the others. I didn't even bother calling them on the radio. I looked over at Phil, but his eyes gave back nothing. I knew what I had to do. I had to go down alone and try to convince them to come back for Phil. I knew he wouldn't last long on his own, not at this altitude. I made Phil as comfortable as possible and put the stove and the little food that was left beside him. He looked right at me, and I sensed a peace, an understanding between us, and I knew that it was okay. He wanted me to go down just as I would want him to go down if the situation were reversed. I tried not to think any more, but the question kept pestering me, I didn't have a choice, did I? *DID I?* I fought back my tears, gave him a squeeze on the shoulder, and said, 'Hang in there, mate.' I turned and left, without my best friend. It was the hardest thing I've ever had to do."

Reflecting on the ordeal his friend had experienced, Gary Scott attributed the tragedy not to Trevor's decision to leave his friend on the mountain but to a much earlier decision—the choice of their climbing partners.

"I've learned not to risk my life with people unless I really know them," Scott explains. "I don't expect others to take risks for me unless I have some history with them. Mark and Steve were part of a climbing team with no history or relationship bonding them all together. They decided not to risk their lives for people with whom they had no long-term relationship or connection. Trevor and Phil made a very costly mistake by choosing to go on an extremely dangerous undertaking without really knowing their teammates."

▲ ▲ ▲

Turning to others involves risks. If we're going to find partners to climb with, one of the risks is that we have to open up to one another, tell our stories, share the brokenness and the pain we carry inside. That's a difficult thing to do if you carry as much shame inside you as Jim was carrying. For him, the years that followed were filled with trial-and-error attempts to find a capable—and trustworthy—climbing partner.

One of the first persons Jim turned to for help was a campus ministry leader who had invited him to be a part of a small-group Bible study. Over time, Jim felt conflicted about the integrity of the ministry and confronted the leader. Instead of discussing Jim's concerns with him, the leader wrote him off as someone "not really committed." These concerns bothered Jim so much that he told the leader he wanted to drop out of the Bible study. In an almost cultish response, the leader said that he couldn't leave the group, that he would be breaking his commitment if he did.

Ironically, the very person who had helped lead Jim to the foot-hills of his faith proved to be the least capable partner for the long climb ahead of him. If Jim couldn't trust him with these concerns, he felt, how could he trust the man with the secrets that were cower-ing within him? In spite of his leader's opposition, Jim left the group. When he did, he left behind some of his innocence. And for the first time in his life, he mistrusted the word *Christian*.

After graduating from college, Jim started going to a large church in the area. Certainly there would be plenty of people there to help shoulder the load he had carried for so long. During this time, Jim was having trouble sleeping. He also suffered from stomach cramps and anxiety attacks. Seeking help, he went to a counselor on the church's staff. The man was good-natured, jovial, and very accepting. Jim liked him, but as it turned out, the man was from the "you-gotta-problem-I-gotta-verse" school of counseling. After listening to each tragic turn in Jim's story, the man merely smiled and turned to a few verses, which he dispensed prescriptively: "Take these and call me in the morning."

With all the smiles and prescriptions and positive attitudes, it was hard for Jim to know if the man had really *heard* his story, if he had made any room in his heart for the pain, the confusion, the tears, the sheer torture of living with a relentless bombardment of blas-phemous thoughts and evil mental images. Leaving the Christian counselor's office, Jim left behind more of his innocence. Now he mistrusted the word *Christian* even more, not only as a noun, but also as an adjective.

Still, Jim didn't give up. He read books, he went on retreats, he listened to tapes, and he attended Bible studies. Desperately searching to find someone who could help, he went on a retreat where his pastor was the speaker. After the session on Friday night, the pastor opened the meeting to questions and answers. Jim listened as people asked several safe questions, ranging from finding a mate to finding out about the end times.

Then came Jim's question.

"Pastor, I've been listening to what you've been teaching about the vine and the branches, about abiding in Christ, about the fruit of the Spirit . . . but I can't honestly say that any of those qualities are present in my life. I don't feel like I possess any of the things you've been talking about. What's more, I can't honestly say that I love God or feel like he loves me. What one thing can you tell me that will make this retreat any different from any of the other retreats and seminars I've been to since I accepted Christ?"

The room went silent as two hundred sets of eyes turned from Jim to the pastor.

It was more than a challenging question; it was a desperate question. Of course, the pastor didn't hear the desperation. All he heard was the challenge. So he entrenched himself, determined to defend his spiritual authority. For the next forty-five minutes, the pastor proceeded to counsel Jim in front of everyone. As the questions he asked became increasingly more personal, the counsel he gave—which he cloaked as compassion—turned into an interrogation.

"I answered every one of them as honestly as I could," Jim told me. "His final question was, 'What is the greatest struggle you have in your life?' After hesitating to get my courage, I answered, 'Purity.' And he jumped all over that. *'I knew it!'* he proclaimed, then pointed at me and said in a loud voice, *'Your problem is rebellion!'* I completely fell apart, sobbing uncontrollably. The pastor had won the battle, and everyone else was in awe of his brilliant insight. He ended with the admonition that I needed to take down the walls I had built, then he prayed for me in front of everyone."

Once again Jim was publicly humiliated. This time, though, it was much worse than the humiliation he had experienced from his brother, his neighbor, his teammates, his coaches, or his sixth-grade science teacher. The humiliation he experienced from the pastor was not merely an echo of those earlier voices; it was a crescendo of those voices, chorusing the refrain "You are a miserable failure, Jim, a shameful excuse for a human being."

The pastor, I believe, was wrong. Rebellion wasn't Jim's problem. Jim was a deeply wounded man. And this leader, instead of drawing near to bind up Jim's wounds the way Jesus would have, stood at a distance and threw salt on them. A healthier person would have left the church. But Jim wasn't a healthy person at that point in his life.

Jim recovered sufficiently and went on to teach Sunday school at the church, something he enjoyed immensely. Over the years the class grew, and so did his confidence. During his stay at the church, a parade of Christian dignitaries came to speak on Sunday mornings. One morning Jim sought out one of the speakers after his sermon.

The man headed an international ministry, and Jim set up an appointment to see if the man could help him find God's will for his life. Jim explained how he hated his job, how he felt God calling him to something, but he didn't know what. After their conversation, the man told Jim he thought his gift was teaching and urged him to go to seminary. Jim followed his advice, enrolling that summer.

It was a conservative seminary, well thought of in the evangelical world. But after a short time there, Jim felt uncomfortable with the evangelical culture. It seemed to him a subtle variation of prosperity theology—simply put, if you knew the truth and obeyed it, your life would run smoothly, your prayers would be answered, and you would live happily ever after. Of course, they didn't say it like that, but to Jim it sounded that way.

Jim later called the man who had encouraged him to go to seminary, telling him he was dropping out. The man asked Jim to work with him in his ministry, which he somewhat reluctantly agreed to do. When the leader learned that Jim had a considerable amount of assets, he encouraged Jim to give his money to the ministry. He even went so far as to set Jim up with an appointment to see a Christian financial planner to show Jim how he could fund his ministry.

When he learned that Jim's family had even more money, he encouraged Jim to talk with them about the possibility of making "generous gifts" to his ministry. Jim recalls those days with sadness. "It seemed to me that everything was about money and power. When I dared to express my concerns, the man attacked my integrity, lecturing me about confidentiality and submission. After a year, I resigned. In spite of the man's charming and persuasive personality, he could be tyrannical. If anyone questioned him, he accused the person of insubordination and usually fired him. As I look back on those days and the people who worked there, it is tragic how many were dumped in the ditch, abused and abandoned in the name of ministry and submission to authority."

As a result of these unfortunate experiences, Jim became more cautious about whom he would confide in. But he continued the climb—in spite of the loneliness, in spite of the disappointments, in spite of how steep it was or how heavy the burden he was carrying.

Along the way, something wonderful happened.

In spite of the frustrating and sometimes hurtful encounters Jim had with numerous counselors, therapists, and church leaders, here and there he met people who were genuinely like Christ, people before whom he could lay down his burdens and find rest. One was a new therapist. Another two were a couple in his church. Another was a leader in the ministry he had joined after dropping out of seminary. Still another was a godly pastor with great counseling skills. And there have been many others he has encountered on the mountain, others who have come alongside him, befriended him, and traveled with him, shouldering some of his burdens.

One of the things that deteriorates for those climbing at high altitudes is their mind. Their thoughts become fuzzy. Their logic breaks down. Their sense of direction gets confused. Something similar happens on the North Face of God. Our thoughts about ourselves begin to break down. When we lose sight of who we are to God, when we forget how dear we are to him, forget how tender his feelings are toward us, we become disoriented. That can be dangerous because it's a slippery slope from self-effacing thoughts to ones that are self-destructive.

A therapist can help pull us back from the precipice. Jim's current therapist is a wonderful Christian man with a great heart. After numerous sessions of patient and empathetic listening, he commended Jim for surviving the abuse as well as he had, going on to say that many individuals with similar backgrounds don't survive. They either commit suicide or die from an unintentional overdose of painkillers.

A big reason they don't survive is the tyranny of their own thoughts. When we experience the silence of God in the midst of our suffering, our interpretation of that silence often adds to the tyranny. For much of his life, Jim was a prisoner of his thoughts. He couldn't imagine that God loved him, let alone delighted in him. He never knew how dear he was to God, how precious the very thought of him was to his heavenly Father. He would sometimes say terrible things to himself about how disgusting he was, how irredeemable he was, how unlovable—things that God would never say.

Fortunately, before he could throw himself off the precipice, Jim found a few men who were willing to climb with him, to carry whatever loads he needed help with, to cut whatever ice was necessary for him to get a foothold, and to hold whatever ropes were necessary to steady him. They are people who enjoy his company, who laugh at his jokes, who listen to his stories—people who love him dearly.

Their love is a reflection of how dearly God loves him.

Slowly but surely he is beginning to see that.

▲ ▲ ▲

For many years Jim searched for some understanding of God's will concerning his life—but he often did it alone. Going it alone is a tendency most of us have. Sooner or later, though, the climb gets harder and more dangerous, and we realize the need for climbing partners.

Our need for help from other people seems to be at least one of the implications of being members of the body of Christ. We need each other *desperately*. We must realize that. And we must realize that needing each other is not our weakness; it is our strength. For it is by God's design that we were made to need each other. To be alone in our search is outside of God's design. To be alone in our struggles, alone in our suffering, cuts us off from a major avenue of God's grace.

In Jim's search for climbing partners, he turned to some who turned on *him*. And so he had to cut the ropes in those relationships, for it was enough to have the gravity of his past working against him without having other people dragging him down. When he cut the ropes, it threw off his equilibrium, and for a while it caused him to stumble. Eventually, though, he regained his balance, pulled to his feet by a few surefooted friends who were willing to take risks with him, believing he was worth the effort.

Since Jim has been in community with a handful of caring Christians, his walk has become more stable and his glimpse of the summit more clear. Still, by his own admission, the long, arduous climb has wearied him, and on any given day he feels like giving up.

I would love to tell you that Jim is now healed and whole and delivered from his demons. He is not. He struggles every day of his life. He struggles with depression. He struggles with the pain of his past. He struggles with his thought life. He struggles with addictions. He struggles with self-worth. He struggles with wanting to keep on struggling, knowing he may spend the rest of his life struggling—and what kind of life is that?

And yet . . .

He loves God—the best he can—and longs to love him even more.

He obeys God—the best he can—and longs to obey him even more.

He serves God—the best he can—and longs to serve him even more.

Of all the things that please God most about Jim, I believe it's the "best he can" and the "even more" that please him most. And perhaps that is what pleases God the most about you and about me when we are struggling to make sense of his silence.

▲ ▲ ▲

While I was doing the final revisions on this book, Jim's therapist arranged for him to have a brain scan in hopes of discovering why no antidepressants had ever worked for him. Jim experienced all of the side effects of the medications but none of the benefits. The scan revealed brain activity consistent with someone who had suffered the trauma of abuse early in life, thus explaining why the medications had not been effective. The doctor who conducted the tests assured Jim that his day-to-day struggles with depression weren't his fault and that help was still available.

This knowledge—even as late as it was in coming—was a parting of the clouds for Jim. And through the clouds, he glimpsed a ray of hope.

It has been a long climb for Jim to get this far. A long and painful climb. With a lot of falls along the way. He has experienced a lot of brokenness and endured a lot of freezing weather. That he even has a relationship with God is remarkable. And that he is able to praise God in spite of all the abuse he has suffered is nothing short of a miracle.

There is a hauntingly beautiful contemporary hymn by Leonard Cohen, titled "Hallelujah." If you've seen the movie *Shrek,* you've heard it. The hymn talks about David's life, his confusion, and his sin with Bathsheba. And then the lyricist integrates his own life into the song, his own joys, his own sorrows, his own struggle to make sense of who God is. Each stanza ends with a chorus of hallelujahs.

The word *hallelujah* comes from two Hebrew words: *hallel,* which means "praise," and jah, which is an abbreviation for Yahweh, or Lord. It literally means "praise the Lord."

In Cohen's hymn, the praise comes from a "baffled" king, its incongruous rhythms rising out of the moral chaos and confusion of his life. Halfway through the song, it says, "Love is not a victory march. It's a cold and it's a broken hallelujah." The final stanza says,

"It's not somebody who's seen the light. It's a cold and it's a broken hallelujah."

When hope and history don't rhyme—especially the hope and history of our own lives—it creates a chasm of opposing realities. The way to bridge that chasm is with our hallelujahs, however cold those hallelujahs feel . . . or however broken.

A PRAYER FOR A CLIMBING TEAM

Dear Lord,

Grant me a climbing team whose legs are strong, whose feet are sure,
*   whose hands are always reaching out, holding on, lifting up.*

Put people in my life I can trust,
*   people I can rely on when the weather of my heart*
*   turns inclemently against me;*
*   people who are not afraid of how dizzying the heights are,*
*   how precarious the footing,*
*   or how thin the air.*

Give me friends with whom I can share breathtaking views
*   as well as heartbreaking falls.*

Thank you, Lord, for the handful of counselors, teachers, and pastors;
*   for the few friends, family members, and coworkers*
*   you have put into my life to guide my steps.*

Give us all the strength to bear one another's burdens,
*   along with a sense of privilege—even a joy in doing so.*

And give me the grace to praise you in the heartbreaks,
*   no matter how cold and broken the hallelujah.*

camp v

▲

Altitude: 22,000 Feet

For the choir director: A psalm of David,
to be accompanied by an eight-stringed instrument.

O LORD, don't rebuke me in your anger
or discipline me in your rage.
Have compassion on me, LORD, for I am weak.
Heal me, LORD, for my bones are in agony.
I am sick at heart.
How long, O LORD, until you restore me?

Return, O LORD, and rescue me.
Save me because of your unfailing love.
For the dead do not remember you.
Who can praise you from the grave?

I am worn out from sobbing.
All night I flood my bed with weeping,
drenching it with my tears.
My vision is blurred by grief;
my eyes are worn out because of all
my enemies.

Go away, all you who do evil,
for the LORD has heard my weeping.
The LORD has heard my plea;
the LORD will answer my prayer.
May all my enemies be disgraced and terrified.
May they suddenly turn back in shame.
PSALM 6

CAMP V IS MIDWAY up the Western Cwm. After a 1952 expedition with a Swiss party, Tenzing Norgay wrote this about his stay there: "For three weeks we lived and worked in the Western Cwm. But the Swiss did not call it that. They had a better name for it: The Valley of Silence. Sometimes, of course, the wind would howl. Once in a while there was a loud roaring as an avalanche fell from the heights above us. But mostly there was just a great snowy stillness, in which the only sounds were our own voices, our own breathing, the crunch of our boots and the creaking of the pack-straps."

In Psalm 6, David turns once again to God, even though it seems his prayers of late have met with only a great snowy stillness. He is in a valley of silence, and he hears nothing except the sound of his own voice and his own breathing. He feels forsaken and forgotten not only by his friends but also by God. He has prayed, he has pleaded, he has cried. And nothing. No explanation from God—not a word, not a sign, not so much as a gesture.

Verses from the psalm indicate that something terrible has happened to David. Exactly what, he doesn't say. But he does say how he feels about it. He feels physically weak and in agony (v. 2), sick at heart (v. 3), worn out from sobbing (v. 6), and stricken with grief (v. 7). From the depths of that pain comes a question: "How long, O Lord, until you restore me?" (v. 3).

You may not be where David was in Psalm 6, but you may be experiencing similar feelings, asking similar questions. "How long, O Lord, until you restore my marriage . . . my relationship with my father . . . my relationship with my daughter . . . my health . . . my financial situation . . . my love for my work . . . my love for you?"

Being able to voice questions like these is therapeutic. Once the anguish is vented, it eases the pressure inside—and, consequently, the pain inside. Knowing that someone cares enough to listen to your lament eases the pain even more.

But where do you go to find someone like that, someone who won't look at your questions as an assault on his faith, who won't scribble prescriptions while you're processing your pain, who won't look down on you from a pious pulpit?

A nearby church? A neighborhood Bible study? A parachurch ministry? A Christian friend?

Those are good places to start. But don't be discouraged if you find that some Christians don't have the patience or the skill or the compassion to handle another person's pain. Sadly, in some of those places the ear is deemed a pretty insignificant part of the body of Christ. In *Life Together,* Dietrich Bonhoeffer's book about Christians in community, he talks about how vital the ear is to the health of that body. He refers to its role as "the ministry of listening."

> *The first service that one owes to others in the fellowship consists in listening to them. Just as love to God begins with listening to His Word, so the beginning of love for the brethren is learning to listen to them. It is God's love for us that He not only gives us His Word but also lends us His ear. So it is His work that we do for our brother when we learn to listen to him. Christians, especially ministers, so often think they must always contribute something when they are in the company of others, that this is the one service they have to render. They forget that listening can be a greater service than speaking.*

To see what "the ministry of listening" looks like, we'll look at Elie Wiesel's account of entering Auschwitz as a fifteen-year-old boy, then being transported from one concentration camp to another.

He lost everything in those camps. His innocence was first. Then his sister, his mother, his father. And finally his faith.

David's cry to God in Psalm 6 when he was surrounded by his enemies could easily have been Elie Wiesel's cry when he was surrounded by Nazi guards. But young Elie didn't cry those words, not publicly anyway. When liberated from Buchenwald in the waning days of World War II, he vowed not to speak of the horrors for at least ten years.

After the war, Wiesel became a journalist, and ten years later, he came to interview Nobel Prize–winning author François Mauriac. Before the interview began, Mauriac spoke about the children of the Holocaust, concluding his remarks with a sigh: "How often I've thought about those children."

To which Elie Wiesel replied, "I was one of them."

That is the moment when Wiesel broke his silence. He shared how, as a young boy, he had lived for God, studied the Talmud, and was dedicated to serving him. He also shared the horrors of the camps. The small faces of innocent children. The dark smoke curling from the chimneys of the crematoriums. The gray ashes flecking the silent skies.

Wiesel told Mauriac of the day he saw the hanging of a young, angelic-looking boy. Behind him, he heard a groan and a man's voice: "Where is God? Where is He? Where can He be now?"

Then he heard another voice, answering from within: "Where? Here He is—He has been hanged here, on these gallows."

That experience plunged Wiesel into an endless night. "That day," he told Mauriac, "I had ceased to plead. I was no longer capable of lamentation. On the contrary, I felt very strong. I was the accuser, and God the accused. My eyes were open and I was alone—terribly alone in a world without God."

As Mauriac reflected on Wiesel's words, he considered the various ways he could have answered him: "And I, who believe that God is love, what answer could I give my young questioner, whose dark eyes still held the reflection of that angelic sadness which had appeared one day upon the face of the hanged child? What did I say to him? Did I speak of that other Jew, his brother, who may have re-

▲

sembled him—the Crucified, whose cross has conquered the world? Did I affirm that the stumbling block to his faith was the cornerstone of mine, and that the conformity between the Cross and the suffering of men was in my eyes the key to that impenetrable mystery whereon the faith of his childhood had perished?"

What answer would *you* have given this young Jew who had just poured out the darkest secrets of his life and the greatest disappointment of his faith? What words do you say? What verses do you quote? What rebuttals do you make?

Here are Mauriac's reflections, along with his response: "We do not know the worth of one single drop of blood, one single tear. All is grace. If the Eternal is the Eternal, the last word for each one of us belongs to Him. That is what I should have told this Jewish child. But I could only embrace him, weeping."

There are moments, and this is one of them, that are too sacred for words. There are holy places within the sanctuary of our conversations where only tears are pure enough to enter.

Sharing the stories that evoke those tears is not an easy thing to do.

And not without its risks.

It's risky to be honest about our discouragement with life and our disappointment with God. People may not listen. Or they may listen for a while and then grow weary of listening. They may distance themselves from us. They may dismiss us with a platitude or demean us with a scolding.

Telling our stories, sharing our sadness, and voicing our questions can be intimidating. It can also be transforming.

Transforming for the person who talks.

Transforming for the person who listens.

Transforming for the entire community.

For Elie Wiesel and François Mauriac, one moment they were strangers, and then Elie shared his story. When he did, the two men embraced. And through the sacrament of tears, a community was formed that transformed strangers into brothers.

A PRAYER FOR COMMUNITY

Dear God,

Help me to break the silence.

Help me to tell the truth of my story,
*   which shame and sadness have held captive.*

Give me the courage to speak,
*   however traumatic the effort, however halting the words.*

Grant me the trembling grace to get through it,
*   however many tears it takes to punctuate it.*

Thank you for the community that forms
*   around the sharing of each other's stories.*

May I be as good a listener
*   as one I would want listening to me.*

Make me quick to hear and slow to speak,
*   and when I do speak, may my words be full of grace,*
*   tender and sensitive and kind.*

Transform the teller in the telling,
*   and the listener in the listening.*

Create community, Lord, a story at a time,
*   and mature that community*
*   into the fullness of the body of Christ.*

CHAPTER SIX

ENDURING
A DARK NIGHT
ON THE MOUNTAIN

For the choir director:
A psalm of the descendants of Korah . . .
to be sung to the tune "The Suffering of Affliction."
A psalm of Heman the Ezrahite.

O LORD, God of my salvation, I cry out to you by day.
I come to you at night.
Now hear my prayer; listen to my cry.
For my life is full of troubles, and death draws near.
I am as good as dead, like a strong man with no strength left.
They have left me among the dead, and I lie like a corpse in a grave.
I am forgotten, cut off from your care.
You have thrown me into the lowest pit, into the darkest depths.
Your anger weighs me down;
with wave after wave you have engulfed me.
Interlude
You have driven my friends away by making me repulsive to them.
I am in a trap with no way of escape.
My eyes are blinded by my tears.
Each day I beg for your help, O LORD;
I lift my hands to you for mercy.
Are your wonderful deeds of any use to the dead?
Do the dead rise up and praise you?
Interlude
Can those in the grave declare your unfailing love?
Can they proclaim your faithfulness in the place of destruction?
Can the darkness speak of your wonderful deeds?
Can anyone in the land of forgetfulness talk about your righteousness?
O LORD, I cry out to you.
I will keep on pleading day by day.
O LORD, why do you reject me?
Why do you turn your face from me?
I have been sick and close to death since my youth.

I stand helpless and desperate before your terrors.
Your fierce anger has overwhelmed me.
Your terrors have paralyzed me.
They swirl around me like floodwaters all day long.
They have engulfed me completely.
You have taken away my companions and loved ones.
Darkness is my closest friend.

PSALM 88

AFTER GEORGE MALLORY'S first expedition to Everest in 1921, he returned to England and promptly signed up for the next year's expedition. Using bottled oxygen this time, he and his 1922 team reached a height of 27,500 feet until trouble with the oxygen tanks forced them down. After regrouping, Mallory led another assault on the summit but again was forced to abandon the climb, this time due to an avalanche that killed seven of the team's porters.

Two years later Mallory, the most accomplished mountaineer of his generation, returned to Everest. It was 1924, and he was thirty-eight years old. This was his third trip, and he knew that because of his age, it would likely be his last. Determined to make it to the top or die trying, Mallory selected Andrew Irvine, a twenty-two- year-old novice, as his partner. A wiser choice would have been Noel Ewart Odell, a geologist with a clear head and strong climbing skills, who was used to climbing without oxygen. Mallory believed, however, that Irvine, with his expertise in bottled oxygen, was a greater asset.

Odell was the last person to see the two climbers alive. After losing visual contact with them, he scoured the summit with his binoculars. "It seemed to look down with cold indifference on me, mere puny man," he noted, "and howl derision in wind-gusts at my petition to yield up its secret—the mystery of my friends."

Over the years the mystery grew to mythic proportions. As the myth grew, so did the questions. How did they die? Did they fall? Did they freeze to death? Did their oxygen give out? Or was it their strength? And the most nagging question of all: Did they make it to the top?

The fate of the two climbers remained a mystery.

Until 1999.

In that year an expedition was launched in hopes of unraveling the mystery. On May 1 six climbers from the Mallory and Irvine Research Expedition fanned out from Camp V, working their way up the ridge of the North Face, a thirty-degree incline over loose rock. At 11:45 AM, at an altitude just below 27,000 feet, one of the searchers, Conrad Anker, spotted something. Out of the corner of his eye he saw a piece of yellow and blue fabric flapping in the wind. When he reached the spot, the fabric proved to be nylon and therefore nothing related to the 1924 expedition. Then, turning to his right, he saw a distinct patch of white about a hundred feet away, its matte finish distinguishing it from the surrounding terrain. He worked his way toward the shape, which he could now see was the figure of a man. As he got closer, he could see from the man's tattered clothing that it wasn't the body of a modern climber. His mind raced with questions: *Is this a dream? . . . Am I really here?* Then he realized that this was why they had come. And this was who they were looking for. *Andy Irvine,* he thought.

He signaled the others with his radio. While waiting for them, he sat beside the body, filled with reverence.

In twenty minutes the others arrived. Thinking it was Irvine's body, one of the members of the team took a smooth piece of shale and started etching the dates of Irvine's birth and death, something of a tombstone to mark the exposed grave. That is when they turned down the collar and found a tag that read: "G. Mallory." Then, on the seam of the arm, they found another tag, this one reading, "G. Leigh Mallory." To everyone's surprise, it was not Irvine they had found; it was Mallory.

The body was like a frozen log, embedded into the side of the mountain. Much of the body had been hollowed out by goraks— large, black ravens that fly at high altitudes seeking food.

▲

The climbers took samples of the clothing and skin and sifted through the pockets for anything that might reveal what had happened. They were looking for the Kodak camera he had brought with him. If he had reached the summit, he certainly would have taken pictures, and so finding the camera would answer that question once and for all. But the camera was nowhere to be found.

There was no evidence that Mallory and Irvine had reached the summit.

But there was also no evidence that they hadn't.

The search team found a tin of beef lozenges, a silk handkerchief, some letters that Mallory had carefully wrapped, a penknife, a small pencil, and several other artifacts that they collected and brought down with them.

One artifact in particular stood out—a pair of goggles. The frames were bent, but the shaded glass was unbroken. It was not the condition of the goggles that intrigued the searchers, however, but rather the *position* of the goggles. They were found not on Mallory's face or near his body but in his pocket.

Which led them all to one conclusion.

Mallory had been climbing after dark.

A sobering piece of the puzzle.

Mallory had been an excellent climber, very possibly the most skilled climber of his generation. He had not climbed alone. And he had roped himself to his partner.

But he made a fateful decision—the decision to climb in the dark.

▲ ▲ ▲

Darkness is a somber chapter in mountain-climbing literature. Darkness must be anticipated, must be prepared for, but most of all it must be endured. A similar type of darkness—this time spiritual—is a theme in the Psalms. Nowhere is that theme more fully developed than in Psalm 88.

The superscription of the psalm reads: "For the choir director: A psalm of the descendants of Korah, . . . to be sung to the tune 'The Suffering of Affliction.' A psalm of Heman the Ezrahite."

Several things strike me about this superscription. It is a deeply personal psalm, whose lyrics were forged on the anvil of affliction. The other thing that strikes me is the note to the choir director, indicating the tune to which the lyrics should be sung. It seems remarkable to me that a tune such as "The Suffering of Affliction" would exist. Apparently it was a common tune, the way "Amazing Grace" is common to us today. And you can see how we might pair that common tune with some uncommon words and make a totally new song.

Even more striking than the prelude is the pathos of the psalm. Heman the Ezrahite prays and prays and prays, but his prayers go unanswered. He is deserted and despondent—no answer comes. No strong arm of the Almighty is bared to help him. No ray of light comes from heaven to illuminate his circumstances. There is not one word of praise in the psalm. Not one word of thanksgiving. Not one word of hope. And at the end of the psalm it is not God's unfailing love that remains, it is darkness.

The Hebrew word translated "darkness" is *mahshak,* derived from the word *choshek.* It appears only in poetic passages. In verse 6, it refers to the dark place that is the grave. Darkness here is synonymous with death. It is a place where all faith, all hopes, all dreams have been buried.

It is a place we will all come to at some point in our lives.

Walter Brueggemann, in his book *The Message of the Psalms: A Theological Commentary,* says this about the psalm: "Psalm 88 is an embarrassment to conventional faith. It is the cry of a believer (who sounds like Job) whose life has gone awry, who desperately seeks contact with Yahweh, but who is unable to evoke a response from God. This is indeed 'the dark night of the soul,' when the troubled person must be and must stay in the darkness of abandonment, utterly alone."

Even though Heman feels that God has turned his back on him, he doesn't turn his back on God. He cries out, but he cries out to God. He raises questions, but he raises them to God. Brueggemann makes a poignant observation about the psalmist's response: "Psalm

88 shows us what the cross is about: faithfulness in scenes of complete *abandonment*."

I don't know when your dark night on the mountain will come, or how long it will last when it does. I don't have a formula to get you through it . . . or five keys to faithfulness in the midst of complete abandonment . . . or time-tested techniques to help you survive the night.

The darkness strips us of our keys, our formulas, our techniques. It takes them and tosses them down the side of the mountain. And though we feel we can't make the climb without them, the truth is that they were some of the very things that weighed us down and held us back.

▲ ▲ ▲

In 1920 the government of Nepal lifted its ban on foreigners' climbing Mount Everest. A British expedition was mounted in 1921, the first ever from the West. It was a reconnaissance mission to find the most favorable route to the summit for future expeditions. One of the members of that first expedition was George Mallory. Another was C. K. Howard-Bury, who wrote this stunning description of a dawn they experienced on the slopes of Everest:

> Here on this sharp ridge, at a height of 21,000 feet, with no obstruction to hide the view, sunrise came to us in all its grandeur and beauty. To the west, and close at hand, towered up Mount Everest, still over 8,000 feet above us, at first cold and grey, like the dead, and with the sky of the deepest purple behind. Then, all of a sudden, a flash of golden light touched the utmost summit of Mount Everest and spread with a glow of gold all over the highest snows and ridges of this wonderful mountain, while behind the deep purple of the sky changed to orange. Makalu [one of the mountains near Everest] caught next the first rays of the sun and glowed as though alive, and then the white sea of cloud was struck by the rays of the sun and gleamed with colour; then slowly rose and struck against the island peaks in great billows of fleecy white. Such a scene it has

seldom been the privilege of man to see, and once seen leaves a
memory that the passing of time can never efface.

Darkness on Everest is frigid and fraught with danger, so dawn is always a welcome sight. And sometimes, like the time in 1921, it is a sight so spectacular that it blazes forever in memory.

Everyone's night on the mountain is different, both in degree and in duration.

So is everyone's dawn.

I would like to take you through the night that a friend of mine experienced—and into the beginnings of his dawn. He is a man I'll call David, and like the biblical character, he is a man after God's own heart. When I first met him more than thirty-five years ago, he was young and athletic, with a gregarious personality, always smiling, quick with a joke and a pat on the back. He had a social grace about him that put people at ease in his company.

Since birth, David has had a strong calling on his life. When he was born, his father took him and raised him heavenward, dedicating him to God. As David grew, so did his love for God, his love for his family, and his love for the church.

David looked up to his father as a role model, and he grew up hoping to someday have a son who loved him as much as he loved his father. From an early age, David demonstrated strong leadership qualities and was blessed with a remarkable ability to communicate the gospel. He later went to seminary, and after graduating went into full-time youth work. Along the way he married.

Then came the bad news. Because of a congenital defect in his wife's heart, her doctor said that bearing children would be out of the question—a devastating moment for someone who dreamed of having a houseful. Eventually, he and his wife decided to adopt. Then came the good news. The adoption agency notified them that a four-day-old baby boy was waiting for them to take him home from the hospital.

David's dream of being a father had come true.

But when David and his wife brought their son home, they noticed something odd. He was stiff when they held him, and he didn't like to be cuddled. As the baby grew, he was extremely active, easily distracted, and always getting into things. He was also slow in learning to speak, and when he finally did, his speech was impaired. When his son turned four, David and his wife took him to a speech therapist, who determined that the boy not only had language disorders but also learning disorders.

David's son grew up frustrated and angry. Everything was a battle, from breakfast cereals to bedtimes. And the battles were always loud, always draining. He did poorly in school, both academically and socially. At age eight, he went for his first psychological evaluation. They took him again at age ten and for several years thereafter. The list of abnormalities grew with each evaluation. Attachment disorder. Borderline personality disorder. Language disabilities. Learning disabilities. ADHD. Narcissism. And a mild form of autism, known as Asperger's syndrome, that affected his social interactions.

The conclusion of the last psychologist was sobering: "Before he's eighteen, your son will either be in jail or dead."

David and his wife did everything to keep the psychologist's words from coming true. They read books, saw counselors, switched their son from public school to private school to homeschool. Finally they sent him away to a facility for troubled kids. But none of those things helped.

In spite of all the love that David and his wife gave their son, he seemed incapable of loving back. And that broke their hearts. Just when they thought things couldn't get any worse, their son became a teenager. Those years were the worst years of their lives. His rebellion brought them before the authorities of every educational, penal, and mental institution in the area. He was in and out of almost every counselor's office, every jail, every drug and alcohol rehab center.

During this time, David worked at a brokerage firm. As his strength was depleted, so was his performance. He didn't have the heart to talk with the people at work, didn't have the heart to talk at length with clients, didn't even have the heart to go out to lunch with anyone. Instead, he packed a lunch and walked to some quiet place where he ate alone.

During these years, David lived in the Psalms. He didn't want to read the law of Moses. He didn't want to read the Prophets. He didn't want to read the letters of Peter or Paul. Their experience seemed so distant from his. But the Psalms, the Psalms were a pooling of tears, and in their reflection he saw his own furrowed brow, his own bloodshot eyes, his own desperate tears.

During these years, David wrote some psalms of his own, chronicling his thoughts and feelings in his journal. Here are a few of the complaints and questions he cried out to God:

> *You gave me a father's heart and a son who is unresponsive to me.*

> *You called me and trained me. But no prayer, Scripture, church, friend, pastor, or organization has touched my son—if anything, he's worse. . . . How do I reconcile this with your love and your power?*

> *You have teased me with rumor, story, and hearsay. How do I get there from here? How does my son get there?*

> *Your ways seem unfair. Your sentence is too harsh and too long. I'm trapped, helpless, and powerless. And so is my son.*

Besides David's wife, the one other person who walked with him during these desperate times was a close friend named John. John also had a teenage son who had broken his heart, so he knew something of the pain David was going through. But things were starting to turn around for John's son. And John's spiritual life was going through a turnaround too. He was part of the renewal movement within the evangelical church, and he was seeing God work in some pretty dramatic ways. He bubbled over with excitement, sharing the wonderful things God was doing in people's lives at his church. But God wasn't doing anything in David's life *or* his son's, let alone anything wonderful.

David heard an earful of stories about people being delivered from the grip of demonic forces. And so he prayed, fasted for forty days, claimed the promises of God, and even took his son for deliverance. But nothing worked.

In one of his journal entries, David wrote, "I feel powerless before the forces of evil that rule this world and operate in my own household. I often think that the forces of darkness are more powerful than the God to whom I pray."

Finally, one day after another one of John's stories, David looked at him and said, "I don't want to hear one more come-to-Jesus miracle. Save your stories for someone who cares."

A lesser friend would have walked away. But John didn't walk away. For twenty more years he kept showing up. He and David spent time together, talking together, crying together, praying together, and waiting together for God to act.

In raising their son, David and his wife went through every humiliation that parents could possibly face. They spent all the money they had to help their son. They spent all their time, all their energy. All their faith and all their prayers. And by the time their son moved out, all their resources were depleted.

In his journal, David wrote the following words of resignation:

If God doesn't meet me here in my hurt, doubt, and disappointment, with the reality of the relationship of which I have spoken for a lifetime, then I have nothing to hope for or to speak of.

I am broken, crushed, humbled before a God I don't understand.

I weep and mourn. I have come to the end of myself, my resources, my power. . . . Is this the beginning of you, dear God? I want to know. That's why I'm here. Lead me, guide me, restore me, save me.

During the darkest part of the night, five friends met David at a chapel for a "prayer intervention," as he later described it. "We would like to pray for you," they told him, "if you will let us." He let them, and every Friday for the next year and a half, they met with him at that chapel and prayed. They became good climbing partners for the uncertain terrain that lay ahead.

The prayers and the people who came to pray meant so much to David. He heard something from God through them, but he desperately wanted to hear God speak more directly. So he came up with a plan. He decided to take God hostage. David rode his bicycle five miles in the cold to sit in the prayer chapel and wait God out. He brought his Bible, his broken heart, and his journal. After reading a while, journaling a while, praying a while, he heard God speak.

And what God said was this: "If I never heal your son, if I never speak to you the way you want . . . can I still be your God? Will you still love me, still honor me, still serve me?"

Tears streamed down David's face. "Yes," he said. "Even if you never heal my son, even if you never speak to me in the way I want you to . . . yes, you can *still* be my God. And yes, I will *still* love you, *still* honor you, *still* serve you."

▲ ▲ ▲

A scene in J. R. R. Tolkien's book *The Two Towers* describes Middle-earth in one of its darkest nights. After the forces of good, led by Aragorn, retreat to Helmsdeep, the forces of evil gather outside their walls. The odds against Aragorn and his men are overwhelming. Although Gandalf has promised help from the east at the first light of dawn, there is no sign of him. As far as the eye can see, there is only darkness and the forces massed against them.

> Aragorn looked at the pale stars, and at the moon, now sloping behind the western hills that enclosed the valley. "This is a night as long as years," he said. "How long will the day tarry?"
>
> "Dawn is not far off," said Gamling, who had now climbed up beside him. "But dawn will not help us, I fear."
>
> "Yet dawn is ever the hope of men," said Aragorn.

Although everyone's dark night is different, everyone's way out of the darkness is the same. The only way out of the darkness of night is the coming of the dawn, which is the hope of all who have faced their worst fears in the night.

The dawn that ends your night may be a full-orbed miracle or simply a ray of hope. It may be a revelation from heaven that illuminates your suffering or simply a graying of the horizon that allows you enough light to move on with your life.

The dawn that came to David's life was not a miracle. It was not a ray of hope. It was not a revelation that shed light on his suffering. It was merely a moment that God used to raise a lantern on his soul, dispelling a few of the shadows that had gathered there.

It was not the dawn he had prayed for.

But it was enough light to lead him to yes.

A yes like that is ever the hope of God. And though it may not be the dawn we have been waiting for, it is the dawn *God* has been waiting for.

▲ ▲ ▲

How did my friend David get through his long, dark night on the mountain? How do *any* of us get through it?

With a lot of praying. A lot of tossing and turning. A lot of shivering. A lot of questions. But mostly, with a lot of tears.

"Weeping may last through the night," the psalmist writes, "but joy comes with the morning" (Psalm 30:5).

Which raises the question we all want answered.

How do we get to the morning, to the sunshine, to the joy?

There is only one way.

By waiting for it. We can't hurry the dawn, no matter how anxiously we pace the floor or how impatiently we watch the clock. And so the question is not do we wait or not wait, because waiting is all we can do. The question is, *How* will we wait? Will we wait well . . . or will we wait poorly?

Although we can't choose how long we will wait in the darkness, we can choose how *well* we will wait. I think we all know how to wait poorly, so we don't need *that* explained, but what does it mean to wait well? What does that look like?

It looks like my friend David when he started pursuing photography. That is how God began guiding him to some sublime but soft-spoken truths, how he began restoring his faith, and how he began saving his sanity. It was quiet work, and with the loudness of his son's outbursts, he needed the quiet. It was a solitary place too, and with how tired he was of telling his story, he needed the solitude. It was also manageable work, and with how unmanageable his son was, he needed to be able to have some measure of control over something, even if it was only something as small as a darkroom.

When I visited David's home, he showed me some of his photographs. They were all in black and white. Maybe he needed the clarity that black and white brings to a subject. Maybe he felt a tonal match between his life and the wide spectrum of grays. Who knows? But there seemed a kind of kinship between them.

One photograph was titled "Street Cathedral," a scene of concrete supports under an overpass. There were no people in the photograph, no cars. Just the gray concrete holding up the overpass. In that stark edifice, David saw something sacred, he told me, an undergirding that supports the work of God's Kingdom in his city.

Another photograph was a close-up of grass, delicate but strong. It reminded David of the human spirit, which can be crushed to the ground, yet slowly but resiliently springs back.

And then there was "Out of the Ashes," a photograph of a fallen tree, its bark burned, its branches broken. Yet a sprig of life grew out of it. Against all that nature had thrown at the tree, it had somehow survived. And in that image, David saw a reflection of himself.

Looking at the photographs, I saw many of the things that David saw. But I also saw something else. I saw a man who was waiting for God, longing to hear a word, to catch a glimpse—anything. Bravely and courageously, he had searched all sorts of places, from city streets to country fields. Patiently waiting for the right light. Calmly capturing the image. Cupping his ear expectantly to listen to what God might be whispering to him through those images.

Wendell Berry's collection of Sabbath poems, *A Timbered Choir,*

has the type of images that my friend David would have been drawn
to. One of those images illustrates, I think, what it means to wait
well:

> *Lift up the dead leaves*
> *and see, waiting*
> *in the dark, in cold March.*
>
> *The purplish stems, leaves,*
> *and buds of twinleaf,*
> *infinitely tender, infinitely*
>
> *expectant. They straighten*
> *slowly into the light after*
> *the nights of frost. At last*
>
> *the venture is made: the brief*
> *blossoms open, the petals fall,*
> *the hinged capsules of seed*
>
> *grow big. The possibility*
> *of this return returns*
> *again to the seed, the dark,*
>
> *the long wait, and the light again.*

One of the many things nature teaches us is how to wait. All living
things wait through the chill of night for the dawn. And they wait
through the cold of March for the spring. That is the cycle of physical life: the fragile stem straightening into the light . . . the seed . . .
the dark . . . the long wait . . . and the light again.

That is also the cycle of spiritual life.

As much as we would like it to be different, there is no eternal
sunshine of the soul, no endless spring. Understanding that makes
enduring the darkness easier.

And as much as it may feel like it at the time, there is no eternal night either, no endless winter. Understanding that makes waiting for the dawn easier.

And as we wait, we pray. Our prayers may not hurry the sun, but they will heighten our awareness to what is happening in the darkness. As incongruous as it seems, sacred things happen there. C. S. Lewis noted the paradox when he asked, "Why are so many holy places dark places?" They are holy because, even in the dark of night and the cold of March, God is at work, breaking through the husk around our hearts and bringing life from under dead leaves.

▲ ▲ ▲

After twenty-five years with his brokerage firm, David left to start a benevolent ministry that coordinates churches to help the poor in his city. One reason he did it was to make good on his word to keep serving God. Another reason was because, during those troubled years with his son, he had seen what little help the government had to offer families whose needs were desperate.

Every now and then I will get a letter from him—or some other sacrament of friendship. Once, he framed one of his photographs for me. Sometime later, he sent me a CD by Russell Watson, a young English singer he thought I would like. Another time he sent me a book by my favorite living author, Frederick Buechner. It was Buechner's latest at the time and had just come out.

The book was *Speak What We Feel (Not What We Ought to Say)*. In it, Buechner examines the lives and works of four writers who have greatly influenced him: the poet Gerald Manley Hopkins, the novelist Mark Twain, the essayist G. K. Chesterton, and the playwright William Shakespeare. A melancholy tone pervades the works that Buechner chose to examine, largely because for him the tone rings true to life as he has experienced it. He ends his study with these words:

> *This, in short, is the weight of my own sad times, and listening to these four voices speaking out from under the burden of theirs has*

been to find not just a kind of temporary release, but a kind of
unexpected encouragement.

Take heart, I heard them say, even at the unlikeliest of moments.
Fear not. Be alive. Be merciful. Be human. And most unlikely of all:
Even when you can't believe, even if you don't believe at all, even if
you shy away at the sound of his name, be Christ.

It was in a videocassette David sent me that I first learned the weight
of his own sad times. I saw something of Christ's sorrows in him as
he spoke—something of the broken heart Christ had when he walked
this earth, aching for a prodigal world's return, something of
Christ's tears when he came to Jerusalem that one last time: "O Jerusalem, Jerusalem. . . . How often I have wanted to gather your
children together as a hen protects her chicks beneath her wings,
but you wouldn't let me" (Matthew 23:37).

During the saddest of those times, there were moments when my
friend couldn't believe—didn't believe—even shied away at the sound
of Christ's name. Yet even in his sadness, even in his emptiness, even
in his disillusionment, he was still being Christ—only now it was the
man of sorrows, acquainted with grief.

Maybe the darkness is where we meet that man of sorrows.

Maybe it is the *only* place where we can meet him, the only place
where we can come to know that part of him and to love that part of
him.

A PRAYER IN THE DARK

Dear Lord,

Help me to understand that somewhere on the mountain,
  a dark night will come upon my soul.

Help me to realize how dangerous the darkness is.

One misstep, and I could lose everything:
  my marriage, my family, my reputation,
    my faith, even my life.

Help me make it through the night, Lord.

Though it is hard to praise you right now,
  give me the strength not to curse the darkness
    or you for not hurrying the dawn.

Teach me, I pray, not only to wait for that dawn
  but to wait well.

Take me out in nature to listen to the wisdom you have there,
  waiting like expectant seeds
    for the right heart to fall on.

Grant that mine would be such a heart,
  with rich and receptive soil.

Let the unfurling petals of the flower be my teacher.

Let the rooted patience of the tree be my mentor.

You have said that patience is one of the many fruits of your Spirit.

What an apt image.

Give me patience for the process of how patience is produced in my life—
  first the stem, then the leaf, then the ear, then the full ear.

Give me patience to wait for the dawn, Lord,
  and to realize that even in the darkness you are at work,
    breaking down the husk around the seed of my understanding

and bringing life, new and emerging life
that will have its day in the sun
and share in the companionship of all living things.

Thank you for the many ways you have come to me,
for the many people you have sent to me over the years,
humbling themselves to enter my world.

Thank you for the people who stepped into my life
and made a difference in my life.

Who knows what heartaches they carried inside them when they did?

Thank you that even when they couldn't believe,
even when they didn't believe,
even when they shied away at the sound of your name,
they were still faithful in bearing your image.

Even with their gray hair and battered bodies,
they were still faithful.

Through them I know not only something of the joy
you carried in your heart when you walked this earth,
but something of the sorrow.

Thank you for them, Lord, for because of them,
I not only know you more but love you more.

camp vi

▲

Altitude: 23,000 feet

Rescue me because you are so faithful and good.
For I am poor and needy, and my heart is full of pain.
I am fading like a shadow at dusk;
I am brushed off like a locust.
My knees are weak from fasting, and I am skin and bones.
I am a joke to people everywhere;
when they see me, they shake their heads in scorn.
Help me, O LORD my God!
Save me because of your unfailing love.
PSALM 109:21-26

At this altitude, the average climber exhales more than a gallon of moisture a day, and if that isn't replenished, the body quickly begins to break down. Without being replenished by the truth of God's Word, we could suffer from something similar.

In Psalm 119:25, for example, the psalmist declares:

My soul cleaves to the dust;
Revive me according to Your word. (NASB)

In another psalm, David shows symptoms of something similar to altitude sickness, only his is in the spiritual realm. He is disoriented and on the brink of despair. He feels terrible about himself and seems to be wasting away. He is overwhelmed by his enemies. They have slandered him, said hateful things to him, and sought to destroy him (Psalm 109:1-5). And it has taken its toll.

It is hard seeing David like this—knowing that in his youth he killed a lion with his bare hands; knowing that while he was still too young to be a soldier, he slew a giant with a slingshot; knowing that when he was finally old enough to be a soldier, he put armies to flight by how fiercely he fought.

Now he is a commander of soldiers—but he seems so wounded.

He carries with him not only all the battle scars from all those years of combat but also the pain that lies beneath those scars. A younger David, a stronger David, might have taken his sword and hacked his way to happiness. But not this David—not this time. This David calls to God from his weakness, from the place where he has been wounded.

The picture of David in Psalm 109 reminds me of a scene in Thornton Wilder's *The Angel That Troubled the Waters,* a short play based on a storied tradition of healings that took place at the pool of Bethesda (John 5:2-3). In these hand-me-down stories, an angel would come from time to time to stir up the water in the pool, and the first person into the pool after the disturbance would be healed of whatever disease he or she had.

Wilder uses this tradition as the setting for his story. The play opens with a tatter of humanity fringing the pool, knotted in their own misery, waiting for the angel.

It has been a long wait. It is night, and everyone around the pool is asleep. Suddenly an angel with shimmering wings appears at the top of the steps, robed in a regal gown. As the angel descends the steps, the pool trembles in anticipation.

Meanwhile, a newcomer, who is a physician, has come to the pool with a deep and abiding wound of his own. Although he cannot see the angel standing there, he quietly prays for the angel to stir the water so that he can find release from his pain.

Meanwhile, one of the invalids wakes from a dream of the angel troubling the water and throws himself into the pool. The commotion startles the others, who hurl a volley of hateful words at him for waking them. Dripping wet, the invalid sees the newcomer standing next to him. He chastises the physician for coming to the pool, telling him to go back to his work and leave miracles to those who need them.

The newcomer ignores the man and continues his prayer, pleading for healing so he can be a more effective physician.

Oblivious to the presence of the angel, who moves to the lowest step, the invalid talks to himself. As he does, the angel points his finger to the water, almost touching it. The angel then shows him-self, but only to the newcomer.

"Draw back, Physician, this moment is not for you," the angel says.

"Angelic visitor, I pray thee, listen to my prayer."

"Healing is not for you."

The physician tells the angel how much better he could serve if only he were released from the physical bondage that weighs him down.

The angel tells the physician that he must leave, but the man can't bear the thought of being so close to his healing and it being with-held from him.

The angel stands a moment in silence, as if picking his words carefully.

"Without your wound where would your power be?" he asks at last. "It is your very remorse that makes your low voice tremble into the hearts of men. The very angels themselves cannot persuade the wretched and blundering children on earth as can one human being broken on the wheels of living. In Love's service, only the wounded soldiers can serve. Draw back."

The angel kneels, running his finger through the water, causing it to ripple. A divine wind swells the ripples and splashes them upon the steps. The invalid sees this and throws himself into the pool. Again, the commotion wakes the others, but this time, as the man leaps to the steps, they see that he has been healed. Those around the pool spring to their feet, and pandemonium breaks out. Still invisi-ble to the others, the angel pauses a moment to smile at the celebra-tion, then leaves.

▲ ▲ ▲

When I first read this scene, the angel's words deeply touched the pool of my heart and rippled through me in ever greater circles.

"In Love's service, only the wounded soldiers can serve."

It is a heavenly thought but a troubling one. It troubles me to think that there are some of us who, in spite of our faithfulness and prayers, will never receive the wholeness we have so desperately sought. There are some of us to whom the angel of the Lord will say, "Healing is not for you."

In essence, that is what the Lord says to the apostle Paul in 2 Corinthians 12. In that chapter, Paul talks about being caught up into paradise, where he saw things and heard things so astounding that there were no words to express them (vv. 1-4). Such revelations, he acknowledges, could lead to his downfall.

Imagine, for example, how sought-after you would be as a speaker, writer, or consultant if such revelations had been given to *you*. Imagine how people of power and influence would seek you out, sit at your feet, ask your advice, pay you money. The temptation to exalt yourself or to allow others to exalt you would be almost irresistible.

Yet Paul resists it: "That experience is worth boasting about, but I'm not going to do it. I will boast only about my weaknesses. If I wanted to boast, I would be no fool in doing so, because I would be telling the truth. But I won't do it, because I don't want anyone to give me credit beyond what they can see in my life or hear in my message, even though I have received such wonderful revelations from God" (vv. 5-7).

Paul then talks about being given some kind of wound, which he refers to as a "thorn in my flesh." He doesn't say what the thorn is, but commentators have speculated on a wide range of maladies, from an eye disease that affected his sight and perhaps his appearance, to epileptic fits that came upon him when he was speaking in public. Whatever it was, many agree it was physical in nature. It was, after all, a thorn in the flesh.

I'm sure the thorn was confusing, especially at first. Yet Paul came to a place of clarity about it, both as to who put it there and why. He was certain it was a "messenger from Satan," and he was certain it had been sent to "torment" him (v. 7). Perhaps Satan thought the torment would cause Paul to become disappointed with God for not answering his prayers, to become angry with God for not protecting him, to grow bitter with God about his calling and all the pain that went with it.

The torment must have been excruciating because Paul says, "Three different times I begged the Lord to take it away" (v. 8). *Begged.* A desperate word. The thorn must have been painful, perhaps even humiliating. It may have even hindered him in his work, hinting at the content of his prayers, which may have sounded a lot like the physician's prayer in Thornton Wilder's play: "It is no shame to boast to an Angel of what I might yet do in Love's service were I but freed from this bondage."

The unstated premise is that we would be able to serve God better if we were healed of our wounds, freed from our bondage, restored to our wholeness. And perhaps sometimes we would be. But not always. Who knows how effective we would be if we were healed of our woundedness? Maybe it would increase our service. Then again, maybe it would decrease it. Because we can't know for sure, it seems best to leave the decision to God, who, of all people, *would* know for sure.

God's decision for Paul?

"Draw back, this moment is not for you."

With that refusal, however, came revelation: "My grace is all you need. My power works best in weakness" (v. 9).

We are not always given such clear revelation like Paul's about why our prayers aren't answered. But we are given a clear *example* of how to process our unanswered prayers. We don't know how long Paul's dialogue with God lasted, but we do know that revelation came through it, and through the revelation came resolution. "So now I am glad to boast about my weaknesses, so that the power of Christ can work through me. That's why I take pleasure in my weaknesses, and in the insults, hardships, persecutions, and troubles that I suffer for Christ. For when I am weak, then I am strong" (vv. 9-10).

The strong are tempted to lean on their own strength, their own understanding, their own talent, their own resources. The weak are not so tempted. The weak turn to God because they have no one else to turn to. That's why David turns to him in Psalm 109.

I think of these things—of King David's psalm, of Thornton Wilder's play, of the apostle Paul's prayer—and it brings me back to my friend David, to where he is now and to where some of you may be now. Crowded around some pool. Praying for an angel to trouble the waters. Waiting for your time to be healed.

It is a troubling thought—but a heavenly one—that the greater effectiveness of our lives may not come through our wholeness but through our woundedness. If that is true, perhaps we should draw back from the pool, as Paul did, and let the angel's words ripple through us in ever greater circles of understanding:

> *Without your wound where would your power be? It is your very remorse that makes your . . . voice tremble into the hearts of men. The very angels themselves cannot persuade the wretched and blundering children on earth as can one human being broken on the wheels of living. In Love's service, only the wounded soldiers can serve.*

THE PRAYER OF A WOUNDED SOLDIER

Well, Lord,

Those were not exactly the words I was hoping to hear.

But maybe they were the words I needed to hear.

It is so hard sometimes to know the difference,
*   so hard sometimes to know what to pray for,*
*   and for how long.*

When does a person stop praying for something, Lord?

When does a person stop praying for rescue, for release,
*   for healing, for wholeness?*

On the one hand, Paul tells us to pray without ceasing.

On the other hand, he ceases to pray for his own healing.

You were gracious to reveal to him the reason
*   why you didn't answer his prayers.*

Would it be too much to ask the same for me?

If it is true that "in Love's service, only the wounded soldier can serve,"
*   give me the grace to draw back from the pool*
*   that holds the promise of my healing.*

Give me the faith to believe that your power works best in my weakness
*   and that your grace is sufficient for all my insufficiencies.*

CHAPTER SEVEN

REACHING
A SUMMIT
OF UNDERSTANDING

LORD, remind me how brief my time on
earth will be.
Remind me that my days are numbered—
how fleeting my life is.
You have made my life no longer than the
width of my hand.
My entire lifetime is just a moment to you;
at best, each of us is but a breath.

PSALM 39:4-5

ON MAY 29, 1953, two men, a New Zealander named Edmund Hillary and a Sherpa named Tenzing Norgay, stepped onto the summit of Mount Everest and into history as the first to successfully complete the climb.

Hillary described the final leg of their ascent: "We didn't waste any time. I started cutting steps again, seeking now rather anxiously for signs of the summit. We seemed to go on forever, tired now and moving rather slowly. In the distance I could see the barren plateau of Tibet. I looked up to the right and there was a rounded snowy dome. It must be the summit! We drew closer together as Tenzing brought in the slack on the rope. I continued cutting a line of steps upward. Next moment I had moved onto a flattish exposed area of snow with nothing but space in every direction. Tenzing quickly joined me and we looked around in wonder."

In his autobiography, Tenzing Norgay recalls his view from the summit:

> It was eleven-thirty in the morning, the sun was shining, and the sky was the deepest blue I have ever seen. Only a gentle breeze was blowing, coming from the direction of Tibet, and the plume of snow that always blows from Everest's summit was very small. Looking down the far side of the mountain, I could see all the familiar landmarks from the earlier expeditions: the Rongbuk Monastery, the town of Shekar Dzong, the Kharta Valley, the Rongbuk and East

Rongbuk Glaciers, the North Col, the place near the northeast ridge where we had made Camp Six in 1938. Then, turning, I looked down the long way we ourselves had come: past the south summit, the long ridge, the South Col; onto the Western Cwm, the icefall, the Khumbu Glacier; all the way down to Thyangboche and on to the valleys and hills of my homeland.

Beyond them, and around us on every side, were the great Himalayas, stretching away through Nepal and Tibet. For the closer peaks—giants like Lhotse, Nuptse and Makalu—you now had to look sharply downward to see their summits. And farther away, the whole sweep of the greatest range on earth—even Kangchenjunga itself—seemed only like little bumps under the spreading sky.

You and I, and every believer who has gone before us, are part of the whole sweep of the greatest range on earth—the landscape of faith. The genealogy in the first chapter of Matthew maps a portion of that landscape. Some, like Abraham and David, are giant Himalayan peaks, stretching across the horizon. Others, like Rahab and Ruth, are "little bumps" under the spreading sky. Yet who knows what rain might fall on the small parcel of land that is their life, what trickles might form from the rain, what streams from the trickles? And who knows what travelers might stop at those streams to touch that water to their lips?

A Joshua and Caleb, maybe.

Maybe a Boaz.

And who knows what might come from *them*?

The saving of a nation, perhaps.

Perhaps the saving of a world.

▲ ▲ ▲

Years after his historic Everest ascent, Tenzing Norgay would tell his son, "You can't see the entire world from the top of Everest,

Jamling. The view from there only reminds you how big the world is and how much more there is to see and learn."

The curvature of the earth limits how much we can see, even from the summit of the world's tallest mountain on a clear day. Likewise, from the summit of biblical revelation, we can see the far reaches of the promises made to Abraham and to David, but with respect to the promises made to *us,* the curvature of time limits our seeing beyond the handwidth of our own lives.

Here and there we are given glimpses of those promises the way some of the people in the Bible were given glimpses.

Take Abraham, for example. He was told, "I will multiply your descendants beyond number, like the stars in the sky and the sand on the seashore" (Genesis 22:17). Though he was allowed to hold a few grains of that promise in his hand, he was not allowed to set foot on the seashore. He saw it, but only from a distance (Hebrews 11:13). Like Abraham, we are promised much in the Scriptures, much about God's love for us, his care for us, his answers to our prayers. It has been granted to the generations that flow from us to revel on the seashore of those promises. But for you and me it has only been granted to hold a few of those grains in our hands and to imagine the surf that will one day lap upon the shore.

Joseph is an example of another way in which God reveals the mystery of his ways. Joseph spent most of his life not knowing why God had allowed his brothers to sell him into slavery, why he had allowed him to be brought to a foreign land, why he had allowed him to be falsely accused and thrown into prison. From behind bars, it must have all seemed so unjust. But from the summit of understanding that God later granted him, it all made perfect sense (Genesis 50:20). It was there he learned that the seemingly meandering ways of God weren't simply leading to the shaping of his character but also to the saving of his family (a lineage that led to Christ), preserving them through seven years of famine and prospering them for generations to come.

Job, on the other hand, never reached a summit of understanding. He was given an audience with God but never an answer to his suffering; a divine encounter but not an explanation (Job 38–41). Of course, from our vantage point, we can see that his suffering was the result of a satanic assault. The first chapter of Job tells us that. But Job was not given that chapter. So, for him, the mystery of his suffering remained a mystery throughout his life on earth.

In more recent times, Dietrich Bonhoeffer, the German Lutheran pastor who was sent to a concentration camp and later executed for his participation in a plot to overthrow Adolf Hitler, reached a summit of understanding about life that few on the foothills of Christian experience ever come to. As he was being crushed under the jackbooted heel of the Third Reich, he reflected on his life, which seemed like so many inconsequential fragments lying in the dirt.

Months before his death he wrote, "It all depends on whether or not the fragment of our life reveals the plan and material of the whole. There are fragments which are only good to be thrown away, and others which are important for centuries to come because their fulfilment can only be a divine work. They are fragments of necessity. If our life, however remotely, reflects such a fragment . . . we shall not have to bewail our fragmentary life, but, on the contrary, rejoice in it."

From our brief time on earth, it is hard for us to know which parts of our lives are fragments to be thrown away and which parts are fragments of necessity, reflecting a divine work that may be centuries in the making. It was hard, I'm sure, for Abraham to know or for Joseph or Job.

Harder still for someone like the thief on the cross.

He was a man who had broken the hearts of his parents by squandering his life, one petty theft after another. So much of his life contributed nothing to the work that God was doing in the world. But with the words "Remember me when you come into your Kingdom" (Luke 23:42), everything changed.

When suffering shatters the carefully kept vase that is our lives, God stoops to pick up the pieces. But he doesn't put them back together as a restoration project patterned after our former selves. Instead, he sifts through the rubble and selects some of the shards as raw material for another project—a mosaic that tells the story of redemption.

That one moment in the thief's life was so beautiful in God's eyes that he took it in his hand and pieced it into the grand mosaic. When we stand back and see the mosaic, which has been millennia in the making, we realize that it tells a story of faith and forgiveness. But it is more than that. When we take another step back, we see that it conjoins the story of God's faithfulness to each and every generation—from all that have come before us to all that follow after us.

Who would have thought that ragged thief would turn out to be one of the greatest evangelists the world has ever known? How many people over the centuries—people in prison, people in nursing homes, people in hospice care, given days, maybe hours to live—have recalled the one who asked merely to be remembered and was given paradise? And who knows how many of those people are now in paradise because they turned a defeated head to Christ, the way the thief did, and with tear-filled eyes and trembling lips, said something that sounded a lot like "Remember me too."

Despite how the curvature of time has limited our view, from the summit of biblical revelation we can see the entire span of biblical history and the faithfulness of God in keeping his promises. That is the basis of our hope—not simply for us but also for our children. And our children's children. And all the generations after them, on into eternity.

▲ ▲ ▲

Buddhists see mountains as peaks of consciousness where pure understanding can be found. That is why caves around Everest are full of hermits seeking ultimate enlightenment. Christians look at the world differently. For us, pure understanding is found not in nature but in the God of nature. So we look not to the mountains for our help but to the God who created them. As the psalmist reminds us:

> *I look up to the mountains—*
> *does my help come from there?*

▲

My help comes from the Lord,
who made heaven and earth!
PSALM 121:1-2

Sometimes, though, that help is hard to see. As C. S. Lewis explains, God is in his creation in much the same way that Shakespeare is in his plays. The playwright cannot be found in any one scene, one character, or one line of dialogue. Yet, at the same time, he is everywhere—in every scene, every character, every line of dialogue. So it is on the North Face of God. *Where is he?* we wonder. We look around us, and he is nowhere to be found. And then, when we look with the right eyes, we see traces of him everywhere.

He was there in the strength we had within us to make the climb.

He was there in the faith it took to cross the shaky footbridge that stretched over the crevasse of abysmal circumstances.

He was there in the partner who was roped to us, steadying us as we went.

He was there in the climbing team that accompanied us, bringing different people into our lives at different times to make sure we had the help we needed.

He was there in the dawn to make sure that the darkness didn't overwhelm us.

He was there every step of the way, though not always in the ways we expected.

Along the way God spoke. Perhaps infrequently, though sometimes clearly, the way he did with Abraham. Sometimes providentially, through a lifetime of inscrutable circumstances, as he did with Joseph. And sometimes dramatically, in a divine encounter, as he did with Job.

Sometimes, though, he didn't speak at all. At least not in ways we could discern.

So what are we to make of the silence? What was the sense of it, the wisdom in it, the compassion?

Perhaps the story of the Canaanite woman's encounter with Jesus will help (Matthew 15:21-28). It is one of the more enigmatic passages in Christ's life. It seems so, so—what's the word?—un-Christlike. So unlike the Christ we know or think we know.

Jesus and his disciples left Galilee and headed north to Tyre and Sidon, which were coastal cities, trade cities, and more importantly, *Canaanite* cities—cities full of Gentiles—who were outside the covenant community. When Jesus and his disciples arrived in the region, news of Jesus and his miraculous powers spread throughout those cities, and a desperate mother came to him, hoping for a sympathetic response.

"Have mercy on me, O Lord, Son of David! For my daughter is possessed by a demon that torments her severely."

Although the woman is a Gentile, she is clearly a woman of faith, acknowledging Jesus with the messianic title "Son of David" and addressing him as her "Lord." And could any need be greater than a child held hostage by an enemy that is ruthlessly tormenting her?

Now comes the enigmatic part: "But Jesus gave her no reply, not even a word" (v. 23).

Not even a word.

An Everest of indifference, or so it seems.

The disciples add indignity to the indifference: "Tell her to go away," they said [to Jesus]. "She is bothering us with all her begging" (v. 23).

But what is she begging *for?* Not food for herself. Not money for herself. Not healing for herself. In fact, nothing for herself. She is begging, yes, but she is begging on behalf of her child. Wouldn't you?

Yet in spite of her impassioned pleas, Jesus responded coldly: "I was sent only to help God's lost sheep—the people of Israel" (v. 24).

Instead of turning away, this mother drew closer and threw herself at Jesus' feet, pleading more intensely: "Lord, help me!" (v. 25).

But the Lord *didn't* help her. In fact, he dismissed her, and rudely. "It isn't right to take food from the children and throw it to the dogs" (v. 26).

I don't know about you, but if Jesus had spoken to me like that, I would have turned with my tail between my legs and slinked away. But the woman didn't slink away. Neither did she stand her ground and bark back. Instead, she nuzzled an appeal: "That's true, Lord, but even dogs are allowed to eat the scraps that fall beneath their master's table" (v. 27).

Jesus looked at her, seeing the love brimming in this mother's eyes for her daughter, then saw something else. "Dear woman," Jesus said, "your faith is great" (v. 28).

A scrap from heaven's table then fell her way. "Your request is granted."

And the text tells us "her daughter was instantly healed" (v. 28).

I don't know how to think about such a passage. Or how to feel. It doesn't sound right to me. It certainly doesn't *feel* right. It feels insensitive, indifferent, and rude. But Jesus isn't insensitive, indifferent, and rude, not to the brokenhearted anyway, even if they were Gentiles. He was kind and merciful to a lot of Gentiles. So what is going on here?

The woman is like a lot of people who find themselves on the North Face of God. Desperately searching for the Lord. Daringly approaching him. And doggedly pleading for help.

This passage illustrates the dynamic at work not only for this woman but for all of us who have ever struggled with the silence of God. In the face of what seems to be a cold and indifferent response to her suffering, this mother stands on a frozen slope that she knows leads to the summit of her only hope. She kicks the hard ice with her crampons, hacking steps with her ax, struggling for a secure place to put her foot, and from there to leverage herself to the next foot-hold.

She had to lighten her load to get to where she is. She had to leave a lot of herself behind, a lot of her dignity, a lot of her self-suffi-ciency. But at the end of her harrowing ascent, she reaches the sum-mit. Had she abandoned the climb, her view of God might have been forever clouded by her disappointment with him. But because she didn't abandon the ascent, she reached a summit of under-standing about God.

Frankly, I don't understand the silence in the story. But then, I don't understand the silences in my own story. This much, though, I *do* understand: We should not allow the silence of God to silence *us*, not for long anyway.

We are not responsible for his voice, only for ours. And that is a responsibility he has articulated with great clarity, telling us to ask, to seek, and to knock (Matthew 7:7-8)—and to keep on asking, seek-ing, and knocking (Luke 18:1).

The Canaanite woman is a perfect example of that kind of perse-verance.

I heard of another great example in a story told to me at a Christ-mas party one year.

A friend of my wife's told me about her father and her uncle—her dad's brother. Her father was a devoted Christian, and he loved his brother but could never get him to see the value of the incredible gift that Christ had to offer. Still, he prayed for his brother every day. When my wife's friend was old enough, her father invited her to join with him in praying for her uncle. They prayed for years, and for years nothing happened. One time her father even spent forty days fasting for his brother's salvation. And still nothing happened.

Finally, the daughter grew up and left home. Years later when her father died, something of this woman's faith in the importance of prayer died along with him. Her father had been such a good man, and he had prayed so fervently and so faithfully for his brother. Yet all his efforts seemed so futile now that he was gone. After all, if *he* couldn't get his prayers answered, who could?

Sometime later she heard that her uncle—a longtime smoker—

had contracted cancer. It had spread, but no one knew how far because he had stopped going to the doctor. Who knows why? Fear of his fate? Resignation to his fate? Denial of his fate? Who knows?

When the woman visited him, she found that her uncle was a shell of the man she once knew. When she asked him where he was with Jesus, he shook his head and said he wasn't anywhere with him—that he had done too much in his life and wasn't worthy of Jesus.

Then she told him about the thief on the cross: how much he had done in *his* life, how unworthy *he* was—and yet, in a moment of faith, how he had turned to Jesus and was given paradise.

Her uncle was quiet for a moment, and then with tears streaming down his face, he too turned to Jesus.

Two minutes later, he died.

As my wife's friend left her uncle's house that day, she pondered the events of the afternoon.

Why had she come to visit her uncle at that particular hour on that specific day?

Why had she asked him the question she did?

Why had he been willing to hear the good news that day when every other day of his life he had refused to listen?

I can think of only one answer to all these questions: because someone prayed.

And because they never gave up praying.

As mysterious as it seems, our prayers have the power to live after us. Spanning years, sometimes centuries, even millennia. Reaching across time to take the broken pieces of a person's life and gently place them into what can only be described as a divine work.

A PRAYER FOR UNDERSTANDING

Dear Lord,

Help me to understand that I am part of a divine work
that has been millennia in the making.

Though my place may be small, it is significant;
though fragmentary, it is full of meaning.

I pray that whatever suffering comes to me in this life
would, through your gentle hand, become part of a mosaic
that helps to tell a beautiful story of redemption.

I pray, along with David, that you remind me how brief my time on this earth is.

Remind me that my days are numbered, that my life is fleeing away;
an entire lifetime is just a moment to you,
the whole of human existence but a breath.

Remind me of this too:
that though my life is but a breath,
it is a divine breath
that will one day return to you who first gave it.

Grant me the grace to reach a summit of understanding about my circumstances;
and if not a summit, at least a ledge where I can come to peace with them,
and with the peace . . . find rest.

camp vii

▲

Altitude: 24,000 Feet

A prayer of Moses, the man of God.

Lord, through all the generations
you have been our home!
Before the mountains were born,
before you gave birth to the earth and the world,
from beginning to end, you are God.
You turn people back to dust, saying,
"Return to dust, you mortals!"
For you, a thousand years are as a passing day,
as brief as a few night hours.
You sweep people away like dreams that disappear.
They are like grass that springs up in the morning.
In the morning it blooms and flourishes,
but by evening it is dry and withered. . . .

Seventy years are given to us!
Some even live to eighty.
But even the best years are filled with pain and trouble;
soon they disappear, and we fly away. . . .
Teach us to realize the brevity of life,
so that we may grow in wisdom. . . .

Satisfy us each morning with your unfailing love,
so we may sing for joy to the end of our lives.
Give us gladness in proportion to our former misery!
Replace the evil years with good.
Let us, your servants, see you work again;
let our children see your glory.
PSALM 90:1-6, 10, 12, 14-16

Camp VII lies about a mile away from the summit. But given the fact
that mile is almost vertical, the summit is still a long way off. We're

▲

even farther from home. Every time we crawl into our tent, every time we squeeze into our sleeping bags, every time we melt ice for drinking water, we realize how far away home really is. What we wouldn't give for a home-cooked meal, to sleep in our own bed, to have a roof over our heads instead of the thin nylon that our tent is made of.

Why do we have to experience the discomfort of a foreign place before we can appreciate the comforts of home? Curious, isn't it? C. S. Lewis explores that curiosity as it relates to our eternal home. In *The Problem of Pain*, he writes:

> *The Christian doctrine of suffering explains, I believe, a very curious fact about the world we live in. The settled happiness and security which we all desire, God withholds from us by the very nature of the world: but joy, pleasure, and merriment He has scattered broadcast. We are never safe, but we have plenty of fun, and some ecstasy. It is not hard to see why. The security we crave would teach us to rest our hearts in this world and oppose an obstacle to our return to God: a few moments of happy love, a landscape, a symphony, a merry meeting with our friends, a bath or a football match, have no such tendency. Our Father refreshes us on the journey with some pleasant inns, but will not encourage us to mistake them for home.*

Every sorrow, every tear, every loss, every death reminds us that this is not our home. Every ache and pain whispers to us, "You were made from dust, and to dust you will return" (Genesis 3:19). We long for the promise of security, but we know it's a promise that nothing on this earth can fulfill.

Like the children of Israel, we long for a Promised Land where we will be safe and secure. Certainly Moses, their leader, longed for it. In Psalm 90, the only psalm of Moses recorded in the Bible, he speaks from the perspective of a man looking back on his life, dizzy at how quickly it all sped by, the way a dream dissipates upon waking.

Moses is a realist who seems to be saying that even if we live to a ripe old age, it's precious little time. And even the best of those years

▲

have had their share of pain and sorrow. He is at a point in his life where he longs for the "good old days." He longs for the joy he once had, the satisfaction he once felt, the miracles he once saw. He wants to finish well—and to finish happy.

Moses isn't sure how much time he has left, but he wants to live the rest of his life to the fullest with no regrets. So he asks God to teach him to make the most of it, to give him the skill of living life a day at a time, not only stopping to smell the roses but stopping to study them. For even a flower can impart wisdom if we are willing to drop to our knees and listen.

> *In the morning it blooms and flourishes,*
> *but by evening it is dry and withered. (Psalm 90:6)*

Where *have* all the flowers gone?

Where have all the *years* gone?

The patriarch prays for himself and for his children after him, praying that the song they sing at the end of their lives might be a joyful one; that the misery they have experienced will be balanced out by happy experiences; that the evil years will be replaced with a few good ones.

Not a bad thing to long for. But what he really longs for, I think, is more than that. What I think he longs for is home.

Where *is* home for Moses? Is it the palatial estate in Egypt? Is it the peaceful meadows of his father-in-law's fields? Is it the Promised Land of Canaan?

I don't think so. I think the home he longs for is found in verse one:

> *Lord, through all the generations*
> *you have been our home!*

Imagine it. To have God as our home! *That* is where we are secure and safe. That is where we are happy and at peace. In God's presence. *That* is the home Moses longs for, the one we all long for. And that is the home that the apostle John describes in Revelation 21:3-4:

> I heard a loud shout from the throne, saying, "Look, God's home is now among his people! He will live with them, and they will be his people. God himself will be with them. He will wipe every tear from their eyes, and there will be no more death or sorrow or crying or pain. All these things are gone forever."

Maybe the summit of understanding we long for is not an answer to our questions about suffering. Maybe the summit is that place where the suffering ends—not just *our* suffering but *all* suffering. And where the silence ends too.

Who knows, maybe without the suffering and the silence, we might mistake this inn-along-the-way for home. And if we found our security and happiness here on earth, we might never look for it elsewhere. We might never find God. We might never have a home to miss, let alone one to come home to.

A PRAYER FOR HOME

Dear Lord,

Through all the generations, you have been home to us.

*You have been both the foundation under our feet
    and the roof over our heads.*

*You have been both the walls that protect us
    and the windows that have shown us the wonder of the world beyond.*

*You have been the fireplace that warms us when we are cold
    and the porch that cools us when we are hot.*

You are our shelter, O Lord.

*Everything we have ever longed for, we find in you—
    the security, the safety, the satisfaction;
        the gladness, the goodness, the glory.*

*Help me to see that it is not answers I want;
    it is you,
        before whom all questions die away.*

CHAPTER EIGHT

ARRIVING
AT THE FINAL
QUESTIONS

I am worn out waiting for your rescue,
but I have put my hope in your word.
My eyes are straining to see your promises come true.
When will you comfort me?
I am shriveled like a wineskin in the smoke,
but I have not forgotten to obey your decrees.

PSALM 119:81-83

SOMEONE once said, "You don't conquer Everest; Everest conquers you." Robert Macfarlane, in his book *Mountains of the Mind*, describes the process by which that conquest takes place:

> Most of us exist for most of the time in worlds which are humanly arranged, themed and controlled. One forgets that there are environments which do not respond to the flick of a switch or the twist of a dial, and which have their own rhythms and orders of existence. Mountains correct this amnesia. By speaking of forces greater than we can possibly invoke, and by confronting us with greater spans of time than we can possibly envisage, mountains refute our excessive trust in the man-made. They pose profound questions about our durability and the importance of our schemes. They induce, I suppose, a modesty in us.
>
> Mountains also reshape our understandings of ourselves, of our own interior landscapes. The remoteness of the mountain world—its harshness and its beauties—can provide us with a valuable perspective down on to the most familiar and best charted regions of our lives. It can subtly reorient us and readjust the points from which we take our bearings.

Those who have spent time on the North Face of God come down from the mountain as changed people. Some for the better, some for worse. One of the things that changes is the questions we ask God in our attempts to gain our bearings.

Questions like the ones Catherine Marshall and her family asked in a time of tragedy.

Peter Marshall was an eloquent preacher and one-time chaplain to the U.S. Senate. At the age of forty-six, he died of a heart attack. His untimely death raised a lot of questions. "Why?" his wife, Catherine, asked the Lord. "Why take a man who loves You so much, who is in the prime time of life, whose impact on people *for You* is so great?"

She had a million "whys," she said, but not one of them was answered. Soon after her husband's death, she wrote his biography, *A Man Called Peter.* With the success of the book, a new life opened up to her, and a new vocation. The next decade was filled with books and travel and speaking opportunities. It was a fulfilling time, watching her children grow up and grandchildren born. One of those grandchildren was her namesake: Amy Catherine Marshall. But the day Amy was born, she didn't look right. The doctors immediately ran tests on her. The diagnosis: a rare, genetic, *terminal* disease. She was given five to ten weeks to live.

Catherine was heartbroken. She prayed fervently, as did her family and friends. For a while, it seemed their prayers made a difference. The baby's coloring improved, along with her movement and her appetite. But despite their faith and prayers, Amy Catherine never left the hospital. She died barely six weeks old.

During the months that followed, Catherine fell into the darkest abyss of her life. She was angry, both at God and at her friends and family. She was plagued with guilt. She withdrew from people, even the people she loved. And she stopped speaking, stopped writing. For six months she didn't even write in her journal, something she had been so faithful in doing in the past. She felt cold and indifferent, going through the motions but not really feeling anything or accomplishing anything.

Through a lot of love and patience and kindness shown to her from others, she eventually was pulled out of the abyss. There were people roped to her who wouldn't give up on her, who wouldn't let her faith freeze to death in a crevasse of bitterness. Here is a case where the body of Christ worked the way it was designed to work, belaying her to safety, with the result that a life was restored and returned to service. Catherine Marshall believed that the shattering of her life from the blow of her granddaughter's death was part of God's intricate plan. She believed there was wisdom in it, though from her vantage point she couldn't see it. She came to a place of resignation, where she trusted that all would be made clear in eternity when the glory of the Lord would shine through the broken glass and reveal the stained-glass beauty of his plan. This is how she dealt with the *whys* of her suffering. I think there is a different conclusion she could have come to about the death of her granddaughter, which I will discuss in the final chapter.

▲   ▲   ▲

So many of the *why* questions cannot be answered. This seems to be the message that God was trying to get across to Job, who was asking for—and later *demanding*—answers to his suffering. Job's friends essentially told him that we live in a cause-and-effect universe in which everything that goes wrong can be traced to something *we've* done wrong. The threads of the moral universe and the material universe are so intertwined, they argued, that if you drop a stitch in one, it will ruin the weave in the other.

They insisted that God was just, that the universe he ruled was just, and that if life turned out unjust for someone, it was that person's fault, not the fault of God or the universe. But the Lord rebuked that theology. He told Job's counselors, "You have not spoken accurately about me" and demanded a sacrifice to atone for their error (Job 42:7).

Instead of explaining the problem of evil in general or the evil that befell Job in particular, God asked Job to do some explaining of his own. But it was not the chaos in Job's life that God asked him to explain. It was the cosmos. All of God's questions had to do with the complexity of creation. His point was that finite creatures cannot comprehend the infinite. The fingers of our limited minds don't have the dexterity to grasp the sheerness of the weave in order to isolate the various causal threads. The best we can do is to acknowledge our limitations and bow before the mystery.

Here is how God convinced Job that there even *was* a mystery. Answering him from the whirlwind, God said, "Who is this that questions my wisdom with such ignorant words? Brace yourself like a man, because I have some questions for you" (Job 38:2-3).

Here are some of those questions:

"Does the rain have a father? Who gives birth to the dew?

"Who is the mother of the ice? Who gives birth to the frost from the heavens?

"For the water turns to ice as hard as rock, and the surface of the water freezes.

"Can you direct the movements of the stars—binding the cluster of the Pleiades or loosening the cords of Orion?

"Can you direct the sequence of the seasons or guide the Bear with her cubs across the heavens?

"Do you know the laws of the universe? Can you use them to regulate the earth?

"Can you shout to the clouds and make it rain?" (Job 38:28-34)

Because of the complexity of forces that affect the earth's ecosystem, it is difficult to determine the many causal links to a specific natural disaster, whether the link is a disturbance in the magnetic field surrounding the earth caused by solar flares or a difference in air temperature caused by a slight change in water currents.

Sometimes the causal links are impossible to trace, at least with our unaided minds. One case where a causal connection *has* been established is the Dust Bowl of the 1930s. The immediate cause of the Dust Bowl was a decade-long drought that had a devastating effect upon the southern plains. Kansas, Oklahoma, Arkansas, Texas, New Mexico, and Colorado were particularly hard hit. Record winds whipped across the plains, shearing the thin layer of fertile topsoil and creating drifts of sand that resembled the dunes of the Sahara Desert. Poor agricultural practices deepened the effects of the drought, both in severity and in duration.

Although poor agricultural practices, record winds, and the drought were immediate causes of the Dust Bowl, the ultimate cause was a mystery. And for decades it remained a mystery until NASA scientists, armed with satellite technology and state-of-the-art computers, unraveled it.

Siegfried Schubert of NASA's Goddard Space Flight Center and his colleagues developed a computer model from old ship records to study weather patterns over the past one hundred years. The ship records provided day-by-day readings of water temperatures around the world. What they found was that the Pacific Ocean was cooler than normal during the decade of the Dust Bowl and that the Atlantic was warmer than normal.

What do you guess the difference was? Ten degrees? Twelve degrees? No. It was a few tenths of one degree.

What difference could a few tenths of a degree possibly make?

Plenty. The intermingling of temperatures between the Pacific and Atlantic contributed to weakening the jet stream, causing it to change its course. The conclusion from the Goddard Space Flight Center was this: "The jet stream normally flows westward over the Gulf of Mexico and then turns northward pulling up moisture and dumping rain onto the Great Plains. During the 1930s, this low level jet stream weakened, carrying less moisture, and shifted further south."

Here is how the cycle played out. Less rain meant less evaporation, which meant fewer clouds and therefore less rain. The result? The Great Plains dried up. And the plants, which held the precious topsoil in the grip of their roots, died. With their death, the topsoil was at the mercy of the wind.

The unraveling of this mystery could never have been accomplished by finite, human minds alone. Who, in his wildest imagination, would have thought that a few tenths of one degree difference in ocean temperature could have resulted in such devastation? It took satellite technology and sophisticated computers to make the connection. And should our technology ever be able to answer all the questions God put to Job, he will, I think, come to us in another whirlwind encounter with an entirely new and more complex set of questions.

▲ ▲ ▲

The inscrutable mystery of suffering—either our own or the suffering of someone we love—is a catalyst to our dialogue with God. The more intense the suffering, the more intense the dialogue.

At first, our questions reflect the depth of our pain and the degree of our disorientation. Usually, the questions at the beginning are *why* questions, *where* questions, and *how long* questions.

Why, God? . . . *Why* did you let it happen?

Where were you when it happened? *Where* are you now?

How long before you say something, before you do something?

The sheer cliffs of suffering are unfamiliar and uncertain terrain. We scale them as best we can, and none of us does it very well. As our conversation with God continues, though, our steps become more sure. Here and there we gain a foothold. Now and then we come to some camp where we can rest and acclimatize. And then, when our equilibrium returns, the questions we ask are very different. It takes strength to ask them. And even more strength to answer them. For they are questions we must answer with our lives.

Although we have a right to raise our questions to God, to register our disappointments, and to voice our complaints, we also have a responsibility to listen to *his* questions, *his* disappointments, *his* complaints. Otherwise, it is a monologue, not a dialogue.

Luke 18 illustrates how our questions were meant to change in our dialogue with God. In that chapter, Jesus tells a parable to illustrate that we ought to pray at all times and not lose heart. In the parable a poor widow comes to a judge time and again, pleading for justice. Worn out by the woman, the judge finally relents, granting the woman's request.

Here is the application that Christ draws from this parable: "Learn a lesson from this unjust judge. Even he rendered a just decision in the end. So don't you think God will surely give justice to his chosen people who cry out to him day and night? Will he keep putting them off? I tell you, he will grant justice to them quickly! But when the Son of Man returns, how many will he find on the earth who have faith?" (Luke 18:6-8).

Justice is promised quickly, but as in the case of the woman in the parable, it never comes as quickly as we would like. Only God knows why. Part of the problem lies in the discrepancy between how he views time and how we view it. If a thousand of our years is to him just a day (Psalm 90:4), that creates a rub between his timetable and ours. Another part of the problem in the delay of heavenly help is the opposition here on earth, which we saw earlier in the delay of heavenly help to Daniel (Daniel 10). Yet another part of the problem lies in the fact that there are other concerns besides ours that have to be taken into consideration. Over the centuries, the Israelites prayed fervently for the Messiah to come and bring justice with him. For centuries he didn't come. Finally, Jesus came to this earth, we are told, "in the fullness of the time" (Galatians 4:4, NASB). He came, I believe, as quickly as he could. There were a lot of things that had to reach fruition, both in the spiritual realm and in the natural realm, before he *could* come. He came the very minute he could. He didn't delay, although from our perspective it seems that it took forever. A lot of people died waiting. In the same way, it seems he is delaying his return. After all, he told John—*promised* John—that he was not only coming back, but that he was coming back *quickly* (Revelation 22:20, NASB). However, I believe that his second coming is governed by the same time constraints as his first coming. He will return in the fullness of time—the very minute he can. And not a minute later.

Although God's timing is very much an issue to the woman in the parable—and to us—it is not the *point* of the parable. Instead, the point is found in the *reversal*. The important questions are not the ones we ask God but the one he asks us: "When the Son of Man returns, how many will he find on the earth who have faith?" (Luke 18:8).

The question should not be, Where is the fairness that is due me? but, Where is the faith that is due God? If that is the question he will one day ask us, then it is the question we should ask ourselves *today*.

And, to that question, we should add these:

Where is the love that is due him?

Where is the honor?

The obedience?

In the end, these are the questions that matter. Not so much the questions that call God into account but the questions that call *us* into account.

Justice is God's responsibility. Faith is ours. And nowhere is that illustrated more definitively than on the night when Christ was betrayed. In that darkest of nights that fell upon his soul, Christ pleaded for mercy that wasn't granted, encountered suffering he didn't deserve, asked questions that went unanswered. Even so, he surrendered his will, his rights, his very life into the hands of his heavenly Father, however painful it was to do so. And however puzzling.

From the image that Christ left us, Peter drew this application: "God called you to do good, even if it means suffering, just as Christ suffered for you. He is your example, and you must follow in his steps. He never sinned, nor ever deceived anyone. He did not retaliate when he was insulted, nor threaten revenge when he suffered.

He left his case in the hands of God, who always judges fairly" (1 Peter 2:21-23).

Judging fairly is God's responsibility.

Living faithfully is ours.

C. S. Lewis, in *The Screwtape Letters,* writes imaginary correspondence between an old devil, Screwtape, and a young demon named Wormwood whom Screwtape is mentoring. At the end of one of those letters, Screwtape writes, "Do not be deceived, Wormwood. Our cause is never more in danger than when a human, no longer desiring, but still intending, to do our Enemy's will, looks round upon a universe from which every trace of Him seems to have vanished, and asks why he has been forsaken, and still obeys."

The author of Psalm 119, quoted at the beginning of this chapter, is one of those "dangerous humans" that Screwtape fears. Around him, every trace of God seems to have vanished. The psalmist is faint, his eyes are strained, his body is shriveled, and he is exhausted from waiting. He tosses a question heavenward in hopes that someone up there is listening. But no one up there answers.

Standing at a gaping crevasse between the nearness of God's promises and the remoteness of their fulfillment, the psalmist feels forsaken. And yet, as he looks into the abyss of that ambiguity, he makes a choice. He could have chosen to turn back. He could have chosen to throw himself into the chasm. Instead, he chooses to bridge the ambiguity.

He bridged it with a three-letter word:

But.

He longs for God's salvation, which seems distant . . . *but* . . . he puts his hope in God's word.

He strains to see God's promises come true . . . *but* . . . he clings to God's principles.

He is exhausted from waiting for God's comfort . . . *but* . . . he obeys him.

▲

At some time or another, each of us will stand at the same crevasse where the psalmist stood. Shriveled like a wineskin, exhausted, and waiting for an answer from God. He may answer dramatically, out of some whirlwind, as he did with Job. Or he may answer demurely, in a still small voice, as he did with Elijah. Or he may not answer at all, as King David apparently experienced. In that case, we must wait for the day when the answer will come. But even if the answer does not come today, we still must live today.

The question is *how?* How shall we live today?

Will we live by faith, trusting God's Word that he will not forsake us? Or will we live by sight, trusting the *appearance* that God has forsaken us?

If we put our full weight on our forsakenness, our faith will fall headlong into the abyss. But if we take a step, however tenuous, over the footbridge of faith, we will find that it holds. And as we go forward, we will find it is our forsakenness that falls into the abyss.

A PRAYER TO ARRIVE AT
THE FINAL QUESTIONS

Dear Lord,

As I come knocking on heaven's door with my fistful of questions,
help me not to knock so loudly and so persistently
that I miss the sound of your knock on my door.

If I were to hear that knock, open that door, and invite you in,
what questions would you ask me?
"Where is your memory of all the goodness I have shown you in your life?"
"Where is your faith in me? Your love for me? Your obedience to me?"

Please keep my questions from drowning out yours, Lord.

Help me to come to a place
where I can exchange my why questions for what questions:

Help me to move from "Why did you allow this to happen?" to
"What can I do to cooperate with the good you are wanting to bring out of it?"

Help me to move from "Why don't you do something?" to
"What can I do for someone who is hurting and needs to feel your touch?"

Help me to move from "Why don't you say something?" to
"What can I say to someone in pain that will express your love for them?"

camp viii

▲

Altitude: 26,000 Feet

Give your love of justice to the king, O God,
and righteousness to the king's son.
Help him judge your people in the right way;
let the poor always be treated fairly. . . .

May the king's rule be refreshing like spring rain . . .
like the showers that water the earth. . . .

He will rescue the poor when they cry to him;
he will help the oppressed,
who have no one to defend them.
He feels pity for the weak and the needy,
and he will rescue them.
He will redeem them from oppression and violence,
for their lives are precious to him.
Long live the king!
PSALM 72:1-2, 6, 12-15

There is a place on Mount Everest known as the Death Zone. Essentially, it is the terrain that lies above 26,000 feet, the same altitude as Camp VIII. Above 18,000 feet, there are no permanent settlements anywhere on earth, due to a variety of physical compensations the human body makes at high altitude.

The lungs, for example, expel more carbon dioxide than usual, which throws off the blood's pH balance. To correct the imbalance, the kidneys discharge more water, causing dehydration. At 26,000 feet, the cycle is accelerated. At that altitude, the atmospheric pressure is only thirty percent of what it is at sea level. As a result of being in such thin air, the body takes in only thirty percent of the oxygen it needs to sustain itself. To compensate, the heart races at a resting rate of 123 beats a minute, and the risk of stroke or of capillaries leaking blood becomes compounded. In a desperate struggle for survival, vital organs begin robbing the surrounding tissues of oxygen, and this is when the body begins its final breakdown.

People who find themselves in the Death Zone can't stay there long because they will experience either irreversible damage to their body or death. They have a lot of special needs when they are in that zone. They need water. They need oxygen. And they need help getting down.

People who suffer profound losses in their lives find themselves in a spiritual Death Zone. They too have a lot of special needs when they are at that altitude. They need the water of God's truth, to be sure, but they also need the oxygen of his grace. They need help making their way across the precarious terrain of grief, but they also need our patience when they experience spiritual vertigo, freezing in their tracks, feeling like they can't take another step. One of the ways in which God has ordained to provide this help is through the church.

Sadly, the church is not always well equipped to render aid. In Jim's case, as I mentioned in a previous chapter, the help they offered hurt him more than it helped him. Had it not been for a few caring Christians who eventually came alongside to walk with him, he might have been left to die on the cold upper reaches of his despair.

Like many churches, the one that Jim attended did a lot of things well. It did well with preaching. It did well with programs. But it didn't do well with people in pain. If the pain was short lived, the congregation might rally around with offers of practical assistance. But their patience was limited. They didn't do well with ministering to chronic needs, deep wounds, and prolonged pain.

Who knows why? Maybe it's the culture we've grown up in, with its short attention span. Maybe it's the awkwardness of not knowing what to say when we've run out of verses or not knowing what to do when we've run out of programs. Or maybe we feel it's not our problem but rather a problem for professionals.

I believe we can learn some valuable lessons about how the church should function by looking at the Old Testament institution of the role of the king in Israel's theocracy.

God designed both institutions—the Old Testament kingship and the New Testament church—to mediate his rule on earth. Like the church, the king was to be a reflection of God's character in the work he did. That essentially is what is being asked for in Psalm 72, which is quoted in part at the beginning of this chapter, and which is the only psalm we have that was written by King Solomon.

> *Give your love of justice to the king, O God,*
> *and righteousness to the king's son.*
> *Help him judge your people in the right way;*
> *let the poor always be treated fairly. (vv. 1-2)*

The Hebrew word for justice in this verse is *mishpat,* one of the great theological words of the Old Testament. To shed light on its meaning, I want to take you to two passages in which the word is used in a nontheological way.

In Exodus 26:30, for example, God instructs Moses: "Set up this Tabernacle according to the pattern you were shown on the mountain." The word translated "pattern" is *mishpat,* God had a specific blueprint for the Tabernacle, and it was Moses' responsibility to duplicate on earth the design he had seen in heaven.

In another instance, the word is used in Isaiah 28 in a context that discusses the proper order in which land is cultivated (vv. 23-26). First the farmer plows, cultivating the ground. Then he levels the surface. Finally he plants the seed—dill, cumin, wheat, barley, and spelt—each in its own designated section of land. Verse 26 explains how the farmer arrived at this knowledge. The Hebrew of that verse reads: "He teaches him the proper way, his God instructs him." The word translated "proper way" is the word *mishpat.*

In its most basic sense, *justice* means the proper ordering of things here on earth according to a heavenly pattern. So in the Lord's Prayer, when Jesus prays that his Father's will be done on earth as it is in heaven, he is praying for justice.

Our modern-day associations of the word *justice* are something along the lines of people getting what is coming to them. That is one meaning, but its root meaning is much deeper. A couple of contemporary illustrations may help us understand.

When a chiropractor aligns our vertebrae, she is bringing justice, so to speak, to our spine, bringing everything in harmony according to a larger, skeletal design. Or when a mechanic aligns our tires, he is bringing the tires to justice with the overall design of the car's frame.

Solomon explains what justice looks like in the king's day-to-day responsibilities in Psalm 72:12-14:

> He will rescue the poor when they cry
> to him;
> he will help the oppressed,
> who have no one to defend them.
> He feels pity for the weak and the needy,
> and he will rescue them.
> He will redeem them from oppression and violence,
> for their lives are precious to him.

Imagine what it would be like living under a king like that. It would "be refreshing like spring rain on freshly cut grass, like the showers that water the earth" (v. 6).

Which explains the chant in verse 15: "Long live the king!"

When the King of kings came to earth, that is how he lived his life. When Jesus taught about the Kingdom of Heaven, he was helping people align their lives here on earth according to a heavenly pattern. When he restored the strength to the legs of the paralytic or straightened the back of the bent-over woman, he was bringing justice to their bodies by restoring them to their proper working order. When he cast out demons, he was doing the same, restoring a person to his or her right mind, the way God had designed it to work.

That is why, when Jesus straightened the hand of the deformed man and healed the others who were following him, Matthew tells us that what we are seeing is the fulfillment of Isaiah's prophecy:

▲

Look at my Servant,
whom I have chosen.
He is my Beloved,
who pleases me.
I will put my Spirit upon him,
and he will proclaim justice to the nations.
He will not fight or shout or raise his voice in public.
He will not crush the weakest reed
or put out a flickering candle.
Finally he will cause justice to be victorious.
And his name will be the hope
of all the world.
MATTHEW 12:18-21

The way Jesus brought justice to the world was not through loud proclamations or forceful demonstrations. He did it with the utmost gentleness. He did not fight or shout or even so much as raise his voice. When he saw people who had been battered like a bent reed, he would bind them up, not break them off. When he saw someone whose life was flickering in the wind, he wouldn't pinch his fingers together to extinguish it. Instead, he would cup his hands around the wick to revive its flame.

When Jesus came to this world, it was not in some distant ethereal display, like the aurora borealis. He came to us palpably, in flesh and blood, to live among us as one of us. He comes to us still, most often in the same way; not in some spectacular display but through the flesh and blood of other people.

We who are the body of Christ are his flesh and blood on the earth. What does that say about who we are and why we are here?

We are his eyes, so we can see people with the same compassion that Christ would see them with if he were here.

We are his ears, so we can listen with the understanding he would have.

We are his mouth, so we can speak the words he would speak.

We are his hands, so we can reach out to others the way he would if he were here—to touch them, and with our touch bring some measure of healing to their lives and some hope for the future.

That is what it means to be the body of Christ. That is who we are. And that is why we are here—to reach out to those who are in the Death Zone and bring them safely home.

A PRAYER FOR FAITH

Dear Lord,

Thank you for your church.

Forgive us for not knowing very much about what it means
to be the body of Christ.

Forgive us for our professionalism,
for spending so much time trying to dress up the church
and make it presentable to the world,
respectable to the world,
or worse, marketable to the world.

Forgive us for our perfectionisms as we forgive those who are perfectionistic
against us.

I pray for your will to be done on earth as it is in heaven.

Help me to understand that though I may not be able to align the earth
with your will,
I can align the small part of this earth that is my heart, my mind, and my will.

Align my thoughts so that they become your thoughts, Lord.

Align my ways so that they become your ways.

And align my questions with the questions you would ask me.

Help me to realize that in answering those questions with my life,
I am helping to establish your reign on this earth
and doing my part with great tenderness
to ease the pain of those who are suffering here.

CHAPTER NINE

SURVIVING
THE WORST DAY
ON THE MOUNTAIN

O God, you have taught me from my earliest childhood,
and I constantly tell others about the wonderful things you do.
Now that I am old and gray,
do not abandon me, O God.
Let me proclaim your power to this new generation,
your mighty miracles to all who come after me.

PSALM 71:17-18

I T WAS THE WORST DAY in the history of Everest expeditions.

May 10, 1996.

It was a clear day, and ten expeditions were on the mountain, a perilous number. By afternoon, climbers from three of those expeditions created a traffic jam near the summit. So distracted were they with the logistics of getting up and down the summit, none of them saw it coming.

Audrey Salkeld, an Everest researcher working at Base Camp at an altitude of 17,858 feet, was the first to notice. While taking a break, she stepped out of her tent. What she saw stopped her in her tracks. Sweeping through the lower valleys was what she described as a "tire-dump fire, great billowing lilac clouds racing up from the south."

Minutes later the storm hit, its high winds raking across her camp. The storm ascended the southern slopes and swirled around the northern side on its way to the summit. As it was moving up the mountain, journalist Jon Krakauer was moving down the mountain. Here is what he saw:

> Around 3:30 p.m., I left the South Summit ahead of Mike, Yasuko, and Andy, and almost immediately descended into a dense layer of clouds. Light snow started to fall. I could scarcely tell where the mountain ended and where the sky began in the flat, diminishing

*light; it would have been very easy to blunder off the edge of the ridge
and never be heard from again. And the conditions only worsened as
I moved down the peak.*

Four hours later conditions had deteriorated so much that visibility
was less than a few feet. As angry winds hurled sleet and hail at the
peaks, temperatures plunged to a windchill factor of one hundred
degrees below zero. Documentary filmmaker Matt Dickinson, who
was on the mountain that day, describes those who were at risk:

> *There, in the "Death Zone," more than thirty climbers were fighting
> for their lives. On the northern side, three Indian climbers were
> stranded, exhausted and with their oxygen supplies running out, high
> on the Northeast Ridge. On the southern side, two commercial
> expeditions were strung out between the South Col and the
> summit—the Mountain Madness team led by Scott Fischer, and the
> Adventure Consultants team of Rob Hall.*

Throughout the night the storm galed, pinning some in their tents,
stranding others in disoriented clumps. By morning the three In-
dian climbers were dead. So were five others, including Scott
Fischer and Rob Hall, both experienced guides. A total of eight.
The worst loss of life of any day on the mountain. Three other
climbers narrowly escaped death, and two of the survivors lost several of their extremities to frostbite.

When Jon Krakauer reached the Khumbu Icefall on the morning
of May 13, he broke down, weeping as he had not wept since he was a
small boy.

▲ ▲ ▲

An even greater downpour of tears happened three years later in a
suburban neighborhood of Littleton, Colorado.

April 20, 1999.

It was a clear day in that Denver suburb of 35,000, a clear Tuesday
morning without a cloud in sight, when two seniors at Columbine

High School, Eric Harris, eighteen, and Dylan Klebold, seventeen, came to school late, at 11:14 AM. They came wearing black trench coats, carrying shotguns and semiautomatic weapons, along with an assortment of explosive devices.

A billowing darkness was about to storm the school.

Unknown to the rest of the 1,870 students attending the school that day, April 20, 1999, was the 110th birthday of Adolf Hitler. And this was how Klebold and Harris were going to celebrate: They were going to blow up the school, kill as many people as they could, and then go out in a blaze of glory by killing themselves.

It had all been meticulously planned.

Early in 1998 Harris began keeping a journal, outlining his plans for destroying the school. He and Klebold trained on video games, the more violent the better. As early as June 1998, both boys were building pipe bombs, which they planned to use in the attack.

During their high-school years, Harris and Klebold had been harassed by a number of their classmates. Consumed with anger and bitterness, the two were determined to get even. They bought several guns, built an assortment of bombs, and blueprinted the school, determining which doors they would enter, the halls they would travel, and the rooms they would target. They planned to start in the cafeteria, move through the first-floor hallway, up the stairs, and end their shooting spree in the library.

The arsenal they had accumulated included forty-nine carbon dioxide bombs, twenty-seven pipe bombs, eleven propane-gas bombs, seven other incendiary devices, each using more than forty gallons of flammable liquid, and two bombs that they carried in duffel bags, each with a twenty-gallon fuel tank.

The makings of a massive storm.

The morning of the assault, the two booby-trapped the school with pipe bombs and a propane tank they rigged to explode. They also carried several explosive devices with them.

The storm hit without warning.

A blizzard of bullets.

They burst through the doors of the school, laughing as they ran down the hallways, shooting sometimes indiscriminately, sometimes with premeditated deliberateness. They targeted everyone they hated, and they hated a lot of people. Not only specific people but entire groups. They hated athletes, cheerleaders, blacks, Jews, and Christians.

Especially Christians.

The first calls for help came at 11:21 AM. The response was swift. Ten fire trucks, along with forty-eight rescue vehicles and ambulances screeched into the parking lots, preparing for the worst. Two helicopters circled the school. Police cordoned off the perimeter as SWAT teams swarmed around the doors and windows of the school and waited.

At 11:29, Harris and Klebold entered the library, where students were hiding under tables, waiting for help that never came. Shouting obscenities, the gunmen went from table to table on a reign of terror. They left the library at 11:36, leaving behind ten dead and twelve wounded.

At 11:44, the two returned to the cafeteria, checking to see why the bomb they had rigged there hadn't gone off.

At 11:56, they returned to the library.

A few minutes after noon, the killers turned their guns on themselves.

Two shots, and the storm was over.

Along with the killers, twelve students and a teacher lay dead. Twenty-four other students were wounded. Those who survived were traumatized, some in tears, some in shock, some taken to area hospitals for treatment.

The first of the victims was Rachel Scott, who had been eating lunch outside the school with her friend Richard Castaldo. According to Richard, Harris and Klebold approached them and suddenly opened fire. A spray of bullets hit Richard, one of them severing his spine. Two hit Rachel's legs. One went through her backpack, lodging in her torso. Thinking them dead, the shooters left.

As Richard lay paralyzed, Rachel started dragging herself to safety. Seconds later, the shooters returned.

Harris came up to Rachel, grabbed her by the hair, and asked, "Do you believe in God?"

"You know I do," she said.

"Then go be with him." And he shot her in the head.

▲ ▲ ▲

Around noon on the day of the massacre, Darrell Scott was at an antique outlet in nearby Aurora, loading some items into his pickup when his cell phone rang. It was his fiancée, asking if he had heard the news.

"There's been a shooting at Columbine," she said.

Darrell had a son and a daughter who went there, along with a niece and nephew. He raced to the school, listening to the news on his radio, praying all the way there. "While I was praying," he recounts, "I sensed that God was telling me something. I tried to hear His voice amid the confusion of my thoughts and feelings, but when I focused in, I heard these words again and again in my heart: *This is a spiritual event, a spiritual event.*" For the next forty minutes, he kept hearing those words.

At the scene of the shooting, parents and family were directed to a nearby elementary school to hear news as it unfolded, fill out reports, and wait to be reunited with their children. One by one the buses came, shuttling students from the high school. Darrell searched for Rachel on every one of them, but she was nowhere to be found.

Around three in the afternoon, as he was standing outside, waiting for the next bus, Darrell overheard some students say the name *Rachel.* He questioned them, and one of boys said he had seen Rachel's body outside the school.

"Rachel *Scott?*" Darrell asked.

With tears in his eyes, the boy said yes.

Official word of her death didn't come until 11:00 AM the next day. Darrell spent that night alone, weeping and calling Rachel's name over and over again until there was nothing left but dry, wordless sobs.

The days that followed alternated between excruciating pain and an anesthetizing numbness. The outpouring of support from friends and family was incredible. So was the outpouring of their tears. The

▲

funeral was held on April 24, and it was a tribute to the beauty of Rachel's life rather than a diatribe against the ugliness of violence. People stood and shared their memories of her: they cried, they laughed, they mourned, they celebrated.

The memories people shared were of a young woman who loved God, loved people, and loved life. She had befriended so many, especially the brokenhearted, those whose lives were filled with loneliness or sadness of some kind. She had stood up for a handicapped boy when he was being bullied in the halls. She had eaten lunch with a new girl who was sitting by herself in the lunchroom. She had spread joy everywhere she went—and light. Even in the darkest of places. Even in the hearts of Harris and Klebold, with whom she shared a photo-video class.

Months before April 20, the two gunmen had turned in a violent video, showing their obsession with death and destruction. No one had challenged it. Not their parents. Not the teacher. Not the administration. But Rachel had challenged it. It was obvious to her that a spiritual battle was being fought over their hearts. And she stepped onto the battlefield to join the fight. She talked to them about the video and asked why they would produce something like that. She tried being a light in the darkness. But the darkness did not comprehend it.

CNN televised the funeral service without interruption, attracting the largest audience in its broadcast history, even surpassing the audience for Princess Diana's funeral. The service touched millions.

About a month after the funeral, Darrell woke one morning at 4:30. In his room he felt the physical presence of God. Two Scripture passages came to his mind, and it seemed as if God was speaking to him through them. The first one was from the story of Esther: "I have brought you to the Kingdom for such a time as this" (Esther 4:14). The other was a word from Christ to his disciples: "I will put you before kings and leaders and you will not be afraid of what to say. I will put words in your mouth" (Luke 21:12-15).

In the days that followed, Darrell began feeling a sense of destiny. He remembered the pastor who spoke at Rachel's funeral challenging those there to pick up the torch she had been carrying, not to let it fall, not to let the light of kindness be extinguished from the halls of their high school.

Was God calling Darrell to pick up that torch?

Increasingly, he felt so. Years earlier he had stepped away from full-time ministry, had gone through a divorce, and felt God would never allow him to be in ministry again, at least not in any public way. The stirrings within him scared him, though. He had a great job, great friends, and a safe, predictable life he had control of.

Until that day of the storm—the worst day of his life.

Several days after the early-morning encounter, Darrell sensed God speaking to him again. As he sat on the edge of his bed, he prayed, "God, I want to do whatever You are calling me to do, but I have two requests. I do not want to open my own doors to speaking engagements, and I don't want to wear suits. I prefer comfortable clothes such as jeans."

A few minutes after he finished praying, the phone rang. It was Frank Amedia, a businessman in another state, calling to say that he had been praying for Darrell every day since Rachel's death. Then Frank said two things that changed Darrell's life.

First, he said that he believed the Lord was raising Darrell up to speak to leaders and young people across the country—and he offered his financial support for whatever God was calling Darrell to do.

The second thing Frank said involved a dream he'd had. In the dream, Rachel's eyes were flowing with tears and watering something. Although he couldn't quite make out what her tears were watering, he was certain about the tears. He asked Darrell if the dream meant anything to him. It didn't. Frank gave Darrell his phone number and asked him to call if anything came to him about the dream.

Several days later the sheriff's department released Rachel's backpack, which had been held for evidence because it had a bullet hole through it. Darrell drove to pick it up. Inside was Rachel's journal, which the bullet had passed through before striking her. Darrell wept uncontrollably as he read the pages. When he came to the end, he couldn't believe what he saw. It was a drawing of eyes at the top of the page with tears falling on a rose! Thirteen clear tears.

Twelve for the students who died, Darrell said to himself, *and one for the teacher.*

Darrell sat in his truck for a long time, praying to understand what was happening.

What was happening was that the torch was being passed from daughter to father.

God would not allow the enemy to extinguish it.

As Darrell was processing all of this, he read through Rachel's journals, which chronicled her walk with God through her teenage years. He felt humbled by what he read. Her words brought smiles of remembrance. They brought tears. They also brought a growing conviction that God had had a strong calling on her life.

The journals revealed that she'd sensed God was going to use her to have a ministry that would reach around the world; that somehow her high school would be a part of that outreach; and, most sobering, she'd had a premonition that her life would be cut short.

Darrell explains: "The ways of God are mysterious, but we believe that God sovereignly prepared Rachel for her own death, providing her with an increasingly clear awareness that the end was near."

The killers left behind their own journals, their own videos, even their own Web site. In stark contrast with Rachel's words, their journals were filled with hate, bitterness, and an obsession for revenge.

Darrell talks about the dark battle that was being waged in the halls of Columbine, especially in the heart of the boy who killed Rachel: "I believe that spiritual forces were at work to take Eric to the level of hatred and despair that he experienced. Eric may have not known this at the time, but Satan doesn't always reveal his hand. That's why he is called the great deceiver.

"Spiritual forces of another sort were at work to prepare my daughter for what happened to her. I believe with all my heart that God had His hand on Rachel from the moment she was born until the moment she died."

Columbine is a case study in spiritual blindness. The Harrises and Klebolds, for whatever reason, seemed blind to the darkness within their sons, certainly to the depth of that darkness. The therapist who was treating one of the boys seemed blind to the intensity of the battle that was being waged over him. Classmates seemed blind to the pair's intentions. Teachers seemed blind. The police. A parole officer. Even the law enforcement agents sent to the school the day of the shootings—even they seemed blind, standing outside the school until the shooting was over, as if stumbling in the dark, confused as to what to do.

As remarkable as it seems, Darrell Scott is not bitter, and he doesn't blame anyone, though there is plenty of blame to go around. He forgave the boys who shot his daughter. He forgave their parents, the school officials, and the police. In spite of his pain, in spite of his loss, in spite of his unanswered questions, he was determined to pick up Rachel's torch.

"Everyone wrestles with questions about good and evil," he explained, "asking how God can permit bad things to happen in the world. We continue to wrestle with the same issues, and we certainly don't have all the answers. But in some ways, the losses we have endured have helped us experience a deeper level of trust in God and a more accepting faith that He knows exactly what He is doing."

At first glance, Columbine seems a triumph of the forces of darkness over the forces of light. But a second glance reveals it was not extinguished. That light, though dimly burning in the face of the storm, rallied the forces of good to make sure the darkness would not win the day . . . or rule the days that followed.

▲ ▲ ▲

First glances can be deceptive, both in the spiritual realm and in the physical realm. On another fateful day, May 10, 1996, Beck Weathers, a Dallas pathologist, was caught in another storm, half a world away on Mount Everest. After the blizzard hit, he found himself bunched with several other climbers at the edge of the Kangshung Face. The wind whipped around him. His body temperature dropped. Blinded by the snow, disoriented in the dark, lost, out of oxygen, and out of strength.

His predicament could not have been bleaker. His body went through physical vertigo, spiraling into hypothermia, delirium, and ultimately unconsciousness. Sitting virtually lifeless in the snow, his face encrusted with ice, he couldn't move, let alone make the long and treacherous climb down the mountain. Both hands were completely frozen. His eyes were almost blind. Alongside the body of another ill-fated climber, he was left on that slope . . . to die.

For all intents and purposes, he was already dead.

But the next day, something extraordinary happened. Beck Weathers recounts the ordeal:

> *About four in the afternoon, Everest time—twenty-two hours into the storm—the miracle occurred: I opened my eyes. Several improbable, if not impossible, events would follow in succession. I would stand and struggle alone back to High Camp. Next day I'd stand again and negotiate the Lhotse Face. Then there would be the highest-altitude helicopter rescue ever. Those were the big things. The miracle was a quiet thing: I opened my eyes and was given a chance to try.*

When Beck Weathers showed up at a camp where some of the other climbers had gathered, they were shocked. "I couldn't believe what I saw," Todd Burleson recounted. "This man had no face. It was completely black, solid black, like he had a crust over him. His jacket was unzipped down to his waist, full of snow. His right arm was bare and frozen over his head. We could not lower it. His skin looked like marble. White stone. No blood in it."

No one there thought that Beck would survive the night. To their surprise, he did. To their further surprise, he was not only able to stand but also to walk. He was determined to make it down the mountain, and the others were just as determined to make sure he did. One tenuous step at a time, he made it to 20,000 feet, where a helicopter airlifted him to a hospital. Later, Beck had his right arm amputated halfway below the elbow, four fingers on his left hand,

▲

and his nose. His personal and professional lives were forever altered by that tragic storm. For all that was lost that day on the mountain, the one thing that wasn't lost was his character.

Here is what Lou Kasischke, one of Beck's climbing partners, wrote after visiting him: "It hurts me to see Beck like this: rebuilt nose, facial scars, disabled for life, Beck wondering if he can practice medicine again, and the like. But it was also remarkable to see how a man can accept all this and be ready to move on in life."

Beck didn't blame anyone for what happened. And he didn't give up. He is a professional speaker now, giving seminars about that worst day on the mountain and how he survived it.

And how did he survive it? He explains:

Somewhere in the midst of all this came another shock—my epiphany. Suddenly, my family appeared in my mind's eye—Peach, Bub and Meg. This was not a group portrait or some remembered photo. My subconscious summoned them into vivid focus, as if they might at any moment speak to me. I knew at that instant, with absolute clarity, that if I did not stand at once, I would spend an eternity on that spot.

Beck Weathers's survival is miraculous. So is Darrell Scott's. I believe it was God who opened Beck's eyes. I also believe it was God who gave him the picture he needed to get up and make the long trek down the mountain. But the decision to get up, that was his.

Darrell Scott made a similar decision. I believe God gave him a picture of his daughter's heart through her journals. I also believe that God opened Darrell's eyes to the flower that would grow out of her tears.

Like Beck, Darrell knew that if he didn't get up and get moving, he would die. And God's calling on his daughter's life would die with him. The words and images in Rachel's journals seemed prophetic. If he didn't do something with those words and those images, the enemy would triumph.

Darrell describes the swirl of events that followed: "Soon the people connected with Columbine found themselves at the center

▲

of a media cyclone. The media people treated me with the utmost sensitivity, but for the first month, I participated in interviews and media events in a dreamlike daze punctuated by painful moments of despair."

Despite how paralyzing that slope of despair was, he didn't stay there.

He stood up.

And he took a step.

Like Beck, Darrell didn't blame anyone for what had happened. And he didn't give up. He is a speaker now, giving talks about the sudden storm of violence that caught everyone off guard that tragic day at his daughter's school and conducting seminars on how to prevent it from happening in other schools.

One of the places where Darrell spoke was on *The Oprah Winfrey Show*. As he walked onstage to tape the interview, he saw on the screen a larger-than-life photograph of his daughter. It stopped him in his tracks, and he fell to the floor, sobbing. Oprah came up to him to see if he was okay. He told her he had suddenly remembered something Rachel had told him: "Two years ago, with her head cocked and a twinkle in her eyes, she said, 'Dad, someday you're going to see me on *Oprah*.'"

When he shared that with Oprah, she broke down and wept. And so did many of the people in the audience that day.

In the months ahead, Darrell was interviewed by everyone from Tom Brokaw to Larry King, which gave him the opportunity to share Rachel's story with millions of people. Still, he says, "There was a numbness in everything I did. Nothing mattered to me at all, and it was as if everything in the world had the same bland vanilla taste."

That numbness didn't go away overnight. But with each visit to his daughter's gravesite, where he cried his heart out, his feelings gradually returned. His feelings for life, for God, and for the torch that had been passed to him.

I saw something of the blaze of that torch when I heard him speak at a youth convention, at which a few thousand middle-schoolers had come together for a weekend. He challenged them to live out the message of kindness that Rachel had lived, to pick up the torch she had carried, and to bring that light into the darkness of their classrooms, their lunchrooms, their hallways. When he finished, the kids flocked to the front, answering that call on their lives.

When I think of Darrell's life, Psalm 71 comes to mind, especially verse 18:

> *Let me proclaim your power to this new generation,*
> *your mighty miracles to all who come after me.*

The power that Darrell proclaims is the power of kindness. The miracles are the difference that kindness makes in people's lives and how it can transform an entire generation.

Like Beck, Darrell still has his scars, still bears the pain of all he lost on that worst day of his life.

But he doesn't sit there in his sorrow.

He stands up.

Each and every day he stands up.

And regardless of how numb he feels, regardless of how hurt he feels, regardless of how hard it is, he takes a step in the direction of where God would have him go.

That is how he made it down the mountain, how we *all* make it down the mountain—one tenuous but courageous step at a time.

A PRAYER FOR COURAGE

Dear Lord,

Darkness is everywhere and growing deeper.

In our schools. On our televisions. In our video games. On the Internet.

But mostly the darkness is deepening in our hearts.

How intense is the battle for our hearts, Lord.

Help me to fight with you in the battle for my own heart.

Help me not to harbor anger there,
*   knowing that when I do, I give the devil a place in my life,*
*   a base of operations that he didn't have before.*

Help me to watch over my heart with all diligence,
*   knowing it is from within the heart that*
*   hatred, murders, and all sorts of evil things flow.*

Help me to pick up Rachel's torch,
*   to be a light in the darkness,*
*   to dispel hate with my love,*
*   harshness with my kindness,*
*   bitterness with my forgiveness.*

And may that torch touch the lives of others in such a way
*   as to light something in them that would, in turn,*
*   bring light to the darkness that is deepening in their part*
*   of the world.*

Thank you, Lord, for sharing with me the stories of those
*   who have experienced the worst day of their lives*
*   and somehow survived it.*

Thank you for Beck Weathers and for Darrell Scott.

How hard it must have been for them to stand up
*   and make it down the mountain,*
*   one uncertain step at a time.*

However numb they felt, they didn't sit in the snow, waiting to die.

However hard it was to breathe, they kept breathing.

Instead of giving up, they got up.

Thank you that they did, Lord.

Keep me from sitting slumped in my sorrow,
*   as my life ebbs away in some kind of spiritual hypothermia.*

Open my eyes, Lord. Show me the pictures I need to see,
*   pictures of the people who love me, who need me.*

Tell me the words I need to hear,
*   words of truth about what will happen to me if I sit here.*

Give me the courage to stand
*   and to speak of the miracle of how I survived the storm.*

camp ix

▲

Remember that we are the people you chose long ago,
the tribe you redeemed as your own special possession!
And remember Jerusalem, your home here on earth.
Walk through the awful ruins of the city;
see how the enemy has destroyed your sanctuary.
There your enemies shouted their victorious battle cries;
there they set up their battle standards.
They swung their axes like woodcutters in a forest.
With axes and picks, they smashed the carved paneling.
They burned your sanctuary to the ground.
They defiled the place that bears your name.
Then they thought, "Let's destroy everything!"
So they burned down all the places
where God was worshiped.
We no longer see your miraculous signs.
All the prophets are gone,
and no one can tell us when it will end.

PSALM 74:2-9

Camp IX is the last camp on Mount Everest. It sits at 27,900 feet, only 1,135 feet from the summit. It was here that Edmund Hillary and Tenzing Norgay took their final rest before stepping into the history books. They had come so far and overcome so much. So many others before them had given up the ascent because of storms, because of injuries, because of avalanches, because of the physical toll the altitude took on their bodies. But Hillary and Tenzing found themselves in good shape to make an attempt at the summit.

How their hopes must have soared!

What a contrast between their attitude and the attitude of the psalmist who wrote Psalm 74.

What a contrast in circumstances.

Jerusalem has been destroyed by the Babylonians, and the people of Israel have been led away in chains. Just as the prophet Jeremiah had foretold, the city lies in ruins, and the people are destined for seventy years of captivity (Jeremiah 25:11).

The psalmist bewails God's silence. Although the times are desperate, there have been no reassuring signs from heaven. No prophets to guide the people (Psalm 74:9). In fact, Jeremiah himself has been led away in chains (Jeremiah 40:1).

The psalmist appeals to God to remember his covenant with his people (Psalm 74:2), but all indications are that he has forgotten. He asks God to survey the destruction (vv. 3-8), hoping the scene will arouse his pity. It is as hopeless a scene as one could imagine. Even the holiest place in the city—the Temple—has been destroyed, chopped to pieces and burned to the ground.

So devastated by the destruction was Jeremiah that he wrote a funeral dirge about it, in which he offers last rites not only for the holy city but also for his hopes:

> *I cry out, "My splendor is gone!*
> *Everything I had hoped for from the LORD is lost!"*
> *The thought of my suffering and homelessness is bitter beyond words.*
> *I will never forget this awful time, as I grieve over my loss.*
> LAMENTATIONS 3:18-20

The enemies of God's people have obliterated every trace of him. Everything that was dear to the prophet has been destroyed. The holy city. The sacred Temple. The worship of God. Hope lies among the ruins. Could he ever hope again? Could he even *dare* to hope again?

Can we? As we walk among the ruins of our lives, can we hope that they will ever be rebuilt? When the enemy has trampled all that we hold sacred, when we are left to wander dazed among the rubble, when all our dreams have gone up in smoke, how can hope survive? When a child of ours is brutally murdered, cut down in her youth, how can hope survive such a tragedy? When a spouse destroys the sanctuary of a twenty-year marriage, leaving the family in ruins, how can hope survive such an assault? When a family business goes bankrupt, reducing years of hard work to ashes, and the assets are carried into captivity by creditors, how can hope survive such a loss?

Regardless how sorrowful the song, there is always a stanza, if remembered, that can restore hope. Here is what Jeremiah remembered:

> *Yet I still dare to hope when I remember this:*
> *The faithful love of the LORD never ends!*

His mercies never cease.

> *Great is his faithfulness; his mercies begin afresh*
> *each morning.*
> *I say to myself, "The LORD is my inheritance;*
> *therefore, I will hope in him!"*
> LAMENTATIONS 3:21-24

Jeremiah, known as "the weeping prophet" for all the sorrows he endured, went from having his hopes dashed to daring to hope again to being determined to hope. How did this resurrection take place? Through remembering. He remembered, as he stood among the smoldering remains of everything he once held sacred, that something sacred remained, something upon which he could rebuild his life, his faith, his hope. And it wasn't the quarried stone of the city's foundation. It was the cornerstone of God's character. Three sides of that stone come to mind. God's unfailing love, his mercy, and his faithfulness.

Looking around him, Jeremiah couldn't see so much as a potsherd of hope among the ruins. Before he could look forward with any hope at all, he had to look away from his losses and look up. Seeing the morning sun, which came up every day, regardless of the weather, Jeremiah was reminded of the faithfulness of God's covenant love and the freshness of his compassions—easy things to forget when the sun has been obscured for so long, as it had been during World War II.

When World War II ended, an inscription was discovered on the wall of a cellar in Cologne, Germany, where Jews had hidden from the Nazis. The inscription read:

I believe in the sun even when it is not shining.

I believe in love even when feeling it not.

I believe in God even when He is silent.

No matter how dark the night, how dense the clouds, or how total the eclipse, the sun is still at the center of our solar system, shining. So is God. Even though we can't see evidence of him through a miraculous sign or hear guidance from him through a prophetic voice, he is still there, in the center of all things. And he is still shining!

Here is our hope: that a day is coming when there will be no night, a day when all things will be made new. It will come because God is faithful in keeping his promises, both to his creation and to his covenant people. And here is something of what that day will look like:

> "Then I saw a new heaven and a new earth, for the old heaven and the old earth had disappeared. And the sea was also gone. And I saw the holy city, the new Jerusalem, coming down from God out of heaven like a bride beautifully dressed for her husband. . . .
>
> "And the one sitting on the throne said, 'Look, I am making everything new!'. . .
>
> "No longer will there be a curse upon anything. For the throne of God and of the Lamb will be there, and his servants will worship him. And they will see his face, and his name will be written on their foreheads. And there will be no night there—no need for lamps or sun—for the Lord God will shine on them." (Revelation 21:1-2, 5; 22:3-5)

A PRAYER FOR HOPE

Dear Lord,

Help me to hope again.

Help me to dare hope again.

When my hopes are dashed,
*   help me to realize that my security is not in a place of worship*
*   or in a system of worship.*

It is not in the peace of my circumstances
*   or the prosperity of my surroundings.*

It is not in the strength of the convictions inside me
*   or in the capabilities of the people around me.*

It is in you, O Lord.

Should there come a day when everything I once leaned on for security lies in ruins,
*   help me to lift up my eyes from the ashes and look to you.*

May it dawn on me then that your unfailing love, your faithfulness, and your mercies
*   together make up the cornerstone of hope*
*   upon which I can rebuild my life.*

CHAPTER TEN

REALIZING
THE FORCES PITTED
AGAINST US

They lurk in ambush in the villages,
waiting to murder innocent people.
They are always searching for helpless victims.
Like lions crouched in hiding,
they wait to pounce on the helpless.

PSALM 10:8-9

SUFFERING is so hard to comprehend. Not the problem of suffering, per se, but the problem of our suffering. For it is not the theological problem that plagues us but the personal one.

Apart from understanding the forces that are pitted against us, it is impossible to make sense of suffering, either in the abstract or the concrete.

Here is the truth of what we are up against or, more precisely, what is up against us. We have an enemy whose entire existence—every waking moment, every thought, every expenditure of energy—is bent on dethroning God and destroying everything that in some way reflects God's character or represents his rule.

Scripture tells us a lot about our enemy. It describes him as the god of this world (2 Corinthians 4:4) and says that the whole world is under his control (1 John 5:19). Under the devil's dark lordship, mighty powers in this dark world and evil spirits in heavenly places help him maintain that control (Ephesians 6:12). He exercises his control with predatory ruthlessness, stalking the earth like a roaring lion looking for someone to devour (1 Peter 5:8). His pursuit of prey is relentless, stopping at nothing except at the boundaries the Lord has established as the limits of his dominion (Job 1:6-12; 2:4-6). He is a murderer and a liar (John 8:44), inciting others to do the same (1 John 3:7-10; 4:1-6). His names betray him. He is called the commander of the powers of the unseen world (Ephesians

2:2), the ancient serpent, the devil, Satan, and the accuser (Revelation 12:9-10).

Every war has its rules of engagement—how the war will be fought, which weapons will not be used, how prisoners of war are to be treated, etc. The spiritual war is no exception. Regrettably, many of those protocols are a mystery to us.

This much, though, is clear: God created the universe to reflect his glory and to fill it with his love. But love, by its very nature, cannot be coerced. It must be chosen. So the gift of free will was necessary to create the atmosphere in which love would be possible.

Although God is sovereign, his decision to create a universe with free will placed limitations on how *invasive* the exercise of his sovereignty could be. Thus, Jesus stands at the door and knocks, but he doesn't break down the door with a battering ram. And if we don't get up to open the door, he stays outside, with tragic consequences to us all.

God's decision to allow everyone in the universe to exercise free will also placed limitations on how *pervasive* the exercise of his sovereignty would be. As a result, the universe, over which God sovereignly reigns, has pockets of resistance within it, where enemies of God rule and their reign of terror goes unopposed.

Just as there have been great awakenings of good in the world where God has seized enemy-held territory and wonderful things happened as a result, there have also been great awakenings of evil where Satan has reclaimed territory and horrible things happened as a result. How else could we understand such outbreaks of evil as the genocide of six million Jews in the Holocaust of the 1940s, the massacre of eight-hundred thousand Tutsis in Rwanda during a scant one hundred days in 1994, the deaths of almost three thousand people in the World Trade Center, or the execution of thirteen people at Columbine High School in 1999?

When God sent Jesus to earth, he sent him into enemy-held territory so that he could destroy the works of the devil (1 John 3:8). Every casting out of demons was a reclamation of enemy-held territory. Every healing was a repatriation of the casualties of war. Every resurrection was a rebuilding of property the enemy had razed.

Here is what you should know about this enemy: He watches us, stalks us, lies in wait for us. He knows your name, as he knows mine. He knows where we live, where we go, and what we do. He knows the names of our kids. He knows where we are vulnerable. And from these facts, he forges a plan of attack (Ephesians 6:11).

Watch your back, Scripture exhorts us (1 Peter 5:8). And watch the backs of those you love (Ephesians 6:18). Prayer is the way we do that. It's the way we tune in to the spiritual realm, heightening our awareness of Satan's strategies.

One of those strategies is accusation—accusations against us that he raises to God, as he did with Job; accusations against God that he raises to us, as he did with Adam and Eve. When times are most desperate in our lives, Satan lays siege to the perimeter of God's character.

"You have no one in heaven," he says to us, "least of all a father. Look up at the heights, at the mountain that is so cold and distant. *That* is your God. *That* is what you love—or thought you loved. *Look* at it. Love it now. Go ahead, try loving it now. It doesn't care about you. It *never* cared about you. It was just a personification of your needs, conjured up from your fears about being alone in the world and your need for security in a random universe.

"Go looking for your deity on those forbidding slopes. Go ahead and see what you find. Make the climb, come back, and tell us about it. Tell us in the subzero weather how warm he is. Tell us in the howling wind how clearly he speaks. Tell us in the blinding snow how surely he leads. Tell us in the thin air how much he fills you. Tell us in the crevasse how much he cares for you.

"*There* is your God. There in the distance. Take what little faith you have left and pray to the mountain. See if it moves.

"Don't talk about the avalanches you have seen, for that is not the mountain moving. That is only the pull of gravity on a shelf of unstable snow. A purely natural phenomenon. The mountain is not moved by your prayers. And it doesn't care about your pain.

"You have been drawn to pictures of its majestic peaks. You have been stirred by the stories of other climbers. You have been enticed by the call to adventure. And where has all that taken you? Look where you are *now.* Cold and alone and in the worst pain of your life.

"Come down from the mountain. Come down and warm yourself by *real* fires, feed yourself with real food. Keep the pictures on the wall, if you like. Keep the stories on the shelf. Keep the memories of the thrill it gave you, if that's what you need.

"Keep all that spiritual stuff enshrined somewhere in your home. If it gives you comfort, look at it in the morning before you go out in the real world. Look at it in the evening when you return. Keep the fantasy alive, if you like. For the sake of the kids. Like Santa Claus. Enjoy the sentiment of the season, but don't take it seriously. Decorate your home with it, but don't depend on it.

"Deceive yourself no longer.

"You don't have a father in heaven.

"All you have is an Everest of indifference."

▲ ▲ ▲

As god of this world, the enemy cannot control our hearts, but he can control the weather that wisps around us. Clouds are everywhere. So is the wind, the cold, and the snow. When our spiritual eyes are blinded by the sleet, when our feelings are frostbitten, when our thoughts are disoriented by the altitude, we are in no shape to make judgments, least of all judgments about God.

Those judgments distort the picture of who God is—with disastrous consequences. When the serpent came to Adam and Eve, he showed them a distorted picture of God. Based on that picture, they turned their backs on their Creator.

If you picture God as an Everest of indifference, the enemy has won the battle for your heart. That was the same battle C. S. Lewis came close to losing when his wife died. "Not that I am (I think) in much danger of ceasing to believe in God," he wrote. "The real danger is of coming to believe such dreadful things about Him. The conclusion I dread is not, 'So there's no God after all,' but, 'So this is what God's really like. Deceive yourself no longer.'"

What we supposed was the North Face of God was merely the steepness of the slopes of a fallen world and the cold realities swirling around it. Although the climbing principles remain the same, the identity of the mountain does not. God is not—and never was—an Everest of indifference, although seen through the sleet of suffering, he sometimes appears to be.

So how do we protect ourselves against such distortion?

By keeping a clear picture of God with us at all times.

And how do we do *that*?

The writer to the Hebrews tells us to look to Jesus, for he "radiates God's own glory and expresses the very character of God" (Hebrews 1:3). If you have seen me, Jesus told his disciples, you have seen the Father (John 14:9).

I can only imagine what it must have been like for the widow of Nain to gaze into the eyes of Christ and in them see his compassion for the loss of her only son; or for John to lean against Christ's chest at the Last Supper and feel the beating of a heart that was about to die for the world he loved; or for the leper who was shunned by everyone to have Christ not just talk with him but also touch him, and with his touch bring healing to his body and hope to his future.

The Word became flesh so we could gaze into eyes brimming with the compassion that God has for us and for the losses we have experienced; so we could feel a heart throbbing with the love he has for us; so we could touch skin tingling with the excitement he has for the wholeness of our lives and the fullness of our futures.

Everywhere Jesus went, he left behind pictures that showed us who God is (John 1:18). And what is the composite of those pictures? A God who sees and who cares. A God who listens and who speaks. Who touches and transforms. A God who calms the wind, stills the waves, and extends his hand to the sinking. A God who heals the sick and raises the dead. Who frees the prisoners, feeds the hungry, blesses the children. A God who came at the greatest personal cost to destroy the works of the devil.

Hardly an Everest of indifference.

▲ ▲ ▲

The enemy also comes before God with accusations against *us*, the way he did with Job. And what do you imagine those accusations would be?

"Does she fear you for nothing? Love you for nothing? Serve you for nothing? Surely she has discovered that there is something in it for her. Take away that something, and see how she fears you then, how she loves you then, serves you then. Let me touch her _____" [you fill in the blank]. Pocketbook? Reputation? Best friend? Physical health? Mental health? Marriage? Children?

"Her children. Yes. Let me touch one of her children."

There are many ways the enemy can touch our children. Disease. Drugs. Depression. Even death. Rebellion is another way the enemy can touch them and take them away. Children can leave home without looking back, as in the story of the Prodigal Son. Or, like the other son in the story, they can stay at home and their hearts be taken away by a critical spirit.

From Adam and Eve's firstborn child, who struck down his brother in the fields east of Eden; to Job's children, who were crushed to death by the collapse of his country estate; to Bethlehem's children, who were slaughtered by Herod—a big part of the enemy's strategy involves children.

The stories I have told about Jim, David, and Darrell all revolve around children.

In Jim's case, I believe the enemy made a preemptive strike on Jim as a child in order to keep him from growing up as a whole person, to prevent him from entering into the fullness of his calling.

In David's case, the enemy attacked David's son to keep him from responding to his father's love. Consequently, the son has not followed in the footsteps of his father's faith, and has nearly destroyed his father in the process.

In Darrell's case, the enemy cut Rachel's life short, attempting to prevent God's calling on her from ever reaching fruition.

There is great sadness in all of these men. Yet somehow, by the mercy of God, they have survived their sadness. Not without cost, certainly. Not without tears. Sleepless nights. Depression.

Their stories would make little sense if we lived in a world that is in full compliance with God's will. But these stories make enormous sense if we realize that we live in a world that is in defiance to God's will, ruled by "the god of this world," Satan himself, along with the sinister forces in his service.

I'm not saying this is true in all cases, but certainly it is true in some cases, that those who have experienced devastating circumstances in their lives have experienced them not from the hand of God, nor from the hand of natural consequences, nor from the hand of a fallen world, but from the hand of the enemy.

When Peter Marshall died at the untimely age of forty-six, his wife, Catherine, couldn't understand why God would do such a thing. After all, Peter loved God so much and was making such an impact for him. But maybe, just maybe, it was *because* he loved God so much, and *because* he was making such an impact for God that Peter Marshall ended up in the crosshairs of the enemy.

When Catherine regained her equilibrium after this staggering blow, she picked up the fallen soldier's flag and advanced the cause for which Peter had fought so valiantly. Seeing her story in the context of war, suddenly the deaths of her granddaughter and her husband do not seem like object lessons from the classroom of a stern cosmic schoolmaster, but rather as strategic blows from a ruthless enemy. Had the enemy also killed Catherine, who knows what other person would have picked up her flag and continued the fight. But if he could have embittered her against God, it might have taken her out of the battle forever.

Who knows how many soldiers have put down their weapons and walked away from the battle because the enemy's attack struck too close, too tender. And who could blame them? Who knows how we would have responded if an incoming missile hit us as directly as it did Catherine Marshall—and as repeatedly.

▲ ▲ ▲

For many people, the idea of Satan is just that—an idea. A dusty theological doctrine, part of ancient history or church history. But not *our* history. After all, the medical community has dispelled so many of the myths about the devil, hasn't it? It has been discovered that the problem is a syndrome, not Satan; a disorder, not demonic activity. We have names for those disorders, therapy for those syndromes, and pills for the illnesses.

The professional age in which we live has influenced our theology; if not in the truth of it, at least in the practice of it. For even if we believe in the existence of the devil, we don't talk about it. And if we do, it's all very hushed, like some embarrassing family secret. If we talk about evil at all, we talk about it abstractly. As a problem, not a person. As a puzzle to be solved, not an enemy to be opposed. The result is that the insidiousness of the person behind the evil is masked by our intellectual discussions.

This is where the imagery found in *The Lord of the Rings* can help us. Nothing I have ever read in a book or seen in a movie unmasks the face of evil as fully and as frighteningly as Tolkien's epic tale. Consider the seductive and sometimes irresistible powers of the Ring, for example. The terrifying presence of the Black Riders and their untiring pursuit. The corruption of Gollum. The betrayal of Saruman. The wastelands of Mordor. The grotesque images of the Orcs, bred only for battle. And the insatiable quest of Sauron to gain dominion over Middle-earth.

Together these images show us so much about our enemy, about the relentlessness of his pursuit, the cunningness of his strategies, the ruthlessness of his attacks.

I see the relentlessness of the enemy in his pursuit of Jim.

I see the cunningness of the enemy in his plans for David.

I see the ruthlessness of the enemy in his attack on Rachel Scott.

An example of the relentlessness of Satan's pursuit can be found in the way the nine Black Riders hunted Frodo in search of the ring that had fallen into his hands. Aragorn tells Frodo that the Black Riders will never stop hunting him. The way the dark riders are portrayed in the movie seems like something from a nightmare, and it reminds me of the way that Satan and his forces have pursued Jim since his childhood. The hooded phantoms ride menacing horses with flared nostrils and flanks sweaty from the pursuit. The hooves of the horses pound the dirt roads, punish the stone bridges, and splash in shallow rivers. I wonder, as Jim does, *Will they ever stop hunting him? Will they ever, ever stop?*

An example of the enemy's cunningness can be seen in the descriptions of Saruman, who claimed lordship over Middle-earth, throwing the land into chaos. He took the Orcs into his service, the Wolf-riders, and the vilest from the race of Men. He is described in the book as "a wizard both cunning and dwimmer-crafty, having many guises. He walks here and there, they say, as an old man hooded and cloaked, very like to Gandalf, as many now recall. His spies slip through every net, and his birds of ill omen are abroad in the sky."

This image, which is similar to the Bible's description of Satan, reminds me of the enemy's cunning attacks on my friend David. Dedicated to the Lord at birth, he was a gifted man with a godly heritage and a great calling on his life. Consequently, he was a threat to the enemy. And so he became a marked man, a man that must be dealt with. And decisively. I can imagine the accusations the enemy brought before God. "Does he love you for nothing? Serve you for nothing? Let me touch his dream, let me take away the one thing he most desires, and see if he loves you then, serves you then."

Tolkien's trilogy is also rife with examples of the enemy's ruthlessness. Here is but one of them, from a battle scene:

> Out of the wreck rose the Black Rider, tall and threatening, towering above her. With a cry of hatred that stung the very ears like venom he let fall his mace. Her shield was shivered in many pieces, and her arm was broken; she stumbled to her knees. He bent over her like a cloud, and his eyes glittered; he raised his mace to kill.

I think of this scene in the context of the evil that stalked the halls of Columbine High School, especially the evil that towered above Rachel Scott, raising its weapon to kill. The killers' actions were so premeditated, so meticulous, and most of all so ruthless. In the same way that cold-blooded Cain was recruited into the enemy's service (1 John 3:12), so were Eric Harris and Dylan Klebold. The jurisdiction of hate over their hearts created a base of operations for the enemy, making the slaughter at Columbine possible.

An apparent triumph for the forces of evil.

There is much pain, much suffering, much sorrow in The Lord of the Rings trilogy. In the end, though, the Dark Lord of the Rings isn't the one who triumphs. It's the lowly hobbit, Frodo, who triumphs, though his triumph comes at great personal cost.

In a sad scene at the end of the story, Frodo says good-bye to his friends. It is then we learn that the wound he received earlier in the story from the sword of the Black Rider has not healed and that it would not heal, ever. Frodo is dying, and the elves have arranged a boat to take him away. Sam takes the news the hardest:

> "But," said Sam, and tears started in his eyes, "I thought you were going to enjoy the Shire, too, for years and years, after all you've done."
>
> "So I thought too, once. But I have been too deeply hurt, Sam. I tried to save the Shire, and it has been saved, but not for me. It must often be so, Sam, when things are in danger: some one has to give them up, lose them, so that others may keep them."

When I read this passage, I think of my friend David, who has been a spiritual father to so many over the years. Those sons have married and have had children of their own, settling into Shires of their own and into homes of their own. From those homes have come great memories, great love, great joy. But not from David's home. His life has gone another way. It is the way of the wounded soldier that Thornton Wilder wrote about—the way of Christ, who gave up so many things so that others may keep them.

David is a deeply wounded man and will likely carry the pain of that wound with him to the end of his days. His greatest desire in life—the desire to be a father to his own son—has been withheld from him.

That is his wound.

One day I believe that wound will be healed. I believe there will be a day in heaven when David will see all the sons he has fathered, and behind them the generations of their sons and daughters who can trace their spiritual lineage to him. On that day, here is what I hope for and pray for: that the crowd will part. And that the person David sees there will be his son. That he will run into David's arms, telling his father how much he loves him. And that they will have an eternity to make up for all that the enemy has robbed them of here on earth.

I hope, I pray, and I believe this will happen.

But I don't know that will happen here, in the Shire. And it breaks my heart to say it because I know David will read this and weep when he does.

I think of him and how much he has endured, and it reminds me of a scene from the movie *The Two Towers*. Frodo and Sam have been climbing the narrow and seemingly endless stairs cut into the steep, rocky incline of Cirith Ungul. Wearied by the climb and dispirited by the climb yet to come, Frodo stops. He is hungry and thirsty. His legs have turned to lead, and his eyes have dimmed of all hope:

> *"I can't do this, Sam."*
>
> *"I know," said Sam, his face softening with his tone. "It's all wrong. By rights we shouldn't even be here. But we are. It's like in the great stories, Mr. Frodo. The ones that really mattered. Full of darkness and danger, they were. And sometimes you didn't want to know the end. Because how could the end be happy? How could the world go back to the way it was when so much bad happened? But in the end, it's only a passing thing, this shadow. Even the darkness must pass. A new day will come. And when the sun shines, it will shine out the clearer. Those were the stories that stayed with you, that meant something. Even if you were too small to understand why. But I think, Mr. Frodo, I do understand. I know now. Folk in those stories had lots of chances for turning back, only they didn't. Because they were holding on to something."*
>
> *"What are we holding on to, Sam?"*
>
> *"That there's some good in the world, Mr. Frodo. And it's worth fighting for."*

At times we all come to the place where Frodo came. Footsore and leg-heavy. Without the hope or the strength to carry on. And we tell ourselves or whoever else will listen, "I can't do this." We look at all that lies behind us and all that lies ahead—the darkness, the danger—and we wonder how in the world the ending to our story can be happy.

There is so much sadness in so many people's lives. The stories are heartbreaking, if only we have the heart to listen to them. I can't begin to tell you how the ones I listened to for this book broke my heart. I think of those stories—Jim's, David's, Darrell's—and I wonder how they have survived them. How could their worlds go back to the way they were when so much bad has happened?

The truth is, they can't. Their worlds can never go back to the way they were.

But here is another truth, and the older I get, the truer it becomes. In the end, as Sam said, it's only a passing thing, this shadow. And even the darkness will pass.

We just don't know when.

Perhaps it won't pass until we do, until we are on the outside of our story, when the presence of the King in all his glory will give light to all that once was so dark and so difficult to understand, so impossible to bear.

We have had lots of chances to turn back, you and I. And at some time or another, we may have turned back. But not for long. Not forever.

Why?

Odds are, it was because we had a Sam Gamgee in our lives. Someone who shared our journey and all the hopes and fears along the way. Our Sam. Someone who fought with us . . . and for us . . . and on occasion fought against us, against the part of us that had given in or given up. Someone who sat down with us, laughed with us, cried with us. Someone who stayed up with us, however long the night, or however dark. Someone who carried us when we could no longer carry ourselves; and carried, too, the heavy burden we had been given to bear. Someone who reminded us that our story mattered, that it meant something. That there's something

▲

worth holding on to—some good in the world, some good in a child, some good in ourselves, some good in God, even though at the time we may not have seen it through the darkness that surrounded us.

That good is worth holding on to.

It's worth fighting for, even dying for. It is a *good* fight, make no mistake about that. But make no mistake that it is still a fight—a *real* fight—and not a figure of speech.

As those loyal to the exiled King, we are the resistance movement. When the King returns, the enemy will fall. And we will be left standing, cheering the King's return. However ragged, we will line the war-torn streets, bearing his image, praising his name, and bowing as he passes by.

Until that time, we wait.

As we wait, we resist.

We resist the enemy by fervently loving the Lord Jesus, by fiercely trusting him, by faithfully serving him. As members of the resistance movement, boldly we pray, bravely we fight. For he is the King. The one, true King. And he's worth fighting for.

Like Aragorn in The Lord of the Rings.

In a scene from *The Return of the King* that brought tears to my eyes, Aragorn is on his horse, rallying the horsemen behind him against the forces of evil gathered against them. And when he speaks, you know you are in the presence of a king. He canters his restive horse along the front lines of his ragged forces and calls out to them.

"I see in your eyes the same fear that would take the heart of me." He pauses, his jaw set with determination. "A day may come when the courage of men fails, when we forsake our friends and break all bonds of fellowship." Then standing tall in his saddle, he shouts. "But it is not *this* day! *This* day we fight!" And with those words he leads the charge against the enemy.

There is a battle that lies before us, before each of us, a battle set in motion before the dawn of time and fought in every generation until the once and future King returns.

Now the fate of our Middle-earth falls on us, on you and on me and on all who bear the name of that King.

The enemy has never been more relentless, never more cunning, never more ruthless. A daunting decision stands between us and that enemy.

We can sheathe our swords in retreat. We can lay down our swords in surrender. We can fall on our swords in despair. Or we can, with the brave who have gone before us, draw our swords and ride with full fury into the enemy's ranks.

A day may come when your courage and mine will fail.

But it will not be *this* day!

A day may come when we forsake our friends and break all bonds of fellowship.

But it will not be *this* day!

This day we fight!

And though we may not win the battle or even survive it, it will be remembered that we did not turn back. It will be remembered that we drew our swords. And that though we died, we died fighting.

His call to battle, still ringing in our ears.

Our battle cry, still warm on our lips.

Then ours will be among the stories that mattered, that meant something—the stories that will give courage and strength to those who come after us, on such a day and at such a time when the fate of their Middle-earth falls upon them.

THE AUTHOR'S PRAYER

Dear Father,

Thank you for these chaptered moments with the reader.

No one knows more than a writer
how inadequate words are
to speak to matters of the heart.

I pray that even the most inadequate of my words
have given a little clarity.

And if not clarity, at least a little company.

I pray that my words have helped to part the clouds
that may have obscured you from them.

Thank you, Lord, that you are not an Everest of indifference,
no matter how distant or detached you sometimes seem.

We all believe in the sun
even when it is not shining.

Help us also to believe in you,
even when you are silent.

And during those times when you are silent,
help us not to be.

Help us to sing hallelujah,
however cold or broken it may be.

Hallelujah!
Hallelujah!
Hallelujah!

ENDNOTES

Frontispiece Quote
Elie Wiesel, *Night* (New York: Bantam, 1960), 2.

Chapter One – Ascending with Our Initial Questions
Lee Hough's prayer is from *Between Heaven and Earth*, Ken Gire, ed. (San Francisco: HarperSanFrancisco, 1997), 59–60.

Patricia Hooper's prayer is from "Prayer," *The Atlantic Monthly*, June 1997, vol. 279, no. 6:97.

Nicholas Wolterstorff's prayer is from his book, *Lament for a Son* (Grand Rapids: Eerdmans, 1987), 80.

The quote that begins, "Man raises himself," is from Wiesel, *Night*, 2–3.

Base Camp
The poetry that Mallory and Irvine read to each other included Coleridge's *Kubla Khan*, Shelley's "Mont Blanc," as well as selections from Thomas Gray and Emily Brontë. Source: Robert Macfarlane, *Mountains of the Mind* (New York: Pantheon, 2003), 265.

Chapter Two – Finding an Accurate Map
The quote by Bono that begins, "He was forced into exile," is from the introduction to *Selections from the Book of Psalms* (New York: Grove, 1999), vii–viii.

The background to the lyrics of U2's songs is found in Niall Stokes, *U2 Into the Heart* (New York: Thunder's Mouth, 2001).

The lyrics to "Peace on Earth" are from U2's CD *All That You Can't Leave Behind*, lyrics by Bono. Produced by Daniel Lanois and Brian Eno (PolyGram International Music Publishing, 2000).

Camp II
The quote that begins, "Is there no music that fits our brokenness?" is from Nicholas Wolterstorff, *Lament for a Son* (Grand Rapids: Eerdmans, 1987), 52.

Chapter Three – Climbing Alone

The quote that begins, "At first the going was easy enough," is from Tenzing Norgay with James Ramsey Ullman, *Tiger of the Snows* (New York: Bantam, 1955), 103–104.

The quote that begins, "The whole face of the mountain," is from Jon E. Lewis, ed., *The Mammoth Book of Eyewitness Everest* (New York: Carroll and Graf, 2003), xxxi–xxxii.

The quote that begins, "I had last seen him," is from Douglas H. Gresham, *Lenten Lands* (New York: Macmillan, 1988), 127.

The quote that begins, "What chokes every prayer," is from C. S. Lewis, *A Grief Observed* (New York: Seabury, 1961; repr., New York: Bantam, 1976), 34–35. Citations are to the Bantam edition.

The quote that begins, "It has been said," is from Gresham, *Lenten Lands*, 132–133.

The quote that begins, "Even Warnie did not know," is from Gresham, *Lenten Lands*, 133.

The quote that begins, "An unmanly weakness by the way," is from Brian Sibley, *C. S. Lewis through the Shadowlands* (Grand Rapids: Revell, 1985; repr., Spire, 1999), 158. Citations are to the Spire edition.

Chapter Four – Looking beyond the Clouds

The quote by Bion can be found in John Bartlett, *Bartlett's Familiar Quotations*, 17th ed., Justin Kaplan, gen. ed. (Boston: Little, Brown, 2002), 86.

Camp IV

The quote that begins, "When I could find the strength," is from Stephen Venables, *Everest: Alone at the Summit* (New York: Thunder's Mouth, 2000), 176.

Chapter Five – Finding a Capable Climbing Team

The quote that begins, "When your life is at stake," is from Gary P. Scott, *Summit Strategies* (Hillsboro, Ore.: Beyond Words, 2003), 80.

The story about Trevor Pilling in his own words is from Scott, *Summit Strategies*, 76–86.

Camp V

The quote that begins, "For three weeks we lived and worked," is from Tenzing Norgay with James Ramsey Ullman, *Tiger of the Snows* (New York: Bantam, 1955), 115.

The quote that begins, "The first service that one owes to others," is from Dietrich Bonhoeffer, *Life Together*, trans. John W. Doberstein (New York: Harper and Row, 1954), 97.

The various quotes from François Mauriac are from the Foreword to Elie Wiesel, *Night* (New York: Bantam, 1960), vii–xi.

Chapter Six – Enduring a Dark Night on the Mountain
The story of Mallory and Irvine is from Jochen Hemmleb, Larry A. Johnson, and Eric R. Simonson, as told to William E. Nothdurft, *Ghosts of Everest: The Search for Mallory & Irvine* (Seattle: Mountaineers, 1999).

The quote that begins, "Psalm 88 is an embarrassment," is from Walter Brueggemann, *The Message of the Psalms: A Theological Commentary* (Minneapolis: Augsburg, 1984), 78.

The quote that begins, "Psalm 88 shows us," is from Brueggemann, *Message of the Psalms*, 81.

The quote that begins, "Here on this sharp ridge," is by C. K. Howard-Bury, from the chapter "Reconnaissance" in *The Mammoth Book of Eyewitness Everest*, ed. Jon E. Lewis (New York: Carroll and Graf, 2003), 53.

The quote that begins "Aragorn looked at the pale stars," is from J. R. R. Tolkien, *The Two Towers* (New York: Ballantine, 1966), 152.

The poem by Wendell Berry was written in 1992 and can be found in his book *A Timbered Choir* (Washington, D.C.: Counterpoint, 1998), 154.

The quote, "Why are so many holy places dark places?" is adapted from C. S. Lewis, *Till We Have Faces: A Myth Retold*, paperback edition (Grand Rapids: Eerdmans, 1956), 249.

The quote that begins, "This, in short, is the weight of my own sad times," is from Frederick Buechner, *Speak What We Feel (Not What We Ought to Say)* (San Francisco: HarperSanFrancisco, 2001), 161.

Camp VI
The various quotes from the play "The Angel That Troubled the Waters" can be found in Thornton Wilder, *The Angel That Troubled the Waters and Other Plays* (New York: Coward-McGann, 1928), 145–147.

Chapter Seven – Reaching a Summit of Understanding
The quote that begins, "We didn't waste any time," is from Sir Edmund Hillary, *View from the Summit* (London: Transworld, 1999; repr., New York: Pocket Books, 2000), 14–15. Citations are to the Pocket Books edition.

The quote that begins, "It was eleven-thirty," is from Tenzing Norgay with James Ramsey Ullman, *Tiger of the Snows* (New York: Bantam, 1955), 164.

The quote that begins, "You can't see the entire world," is from Ed Douglas, *Tenzing: Hero of Everest* (Washington, D.C.: National Geographic, 2003), 41.

The quote that begins, "It all depends on whether or not the fragment," is by G. Leibholz, in "Memoir," an introductory essay in Dietrich Bonhoeffer, *The Cost of Discipleship* (New York: Macmillan, 1959; repr., Touchstone, 1995), 33. Citations are to the Touchstone edition.

Camp VII
The quote that begins, "The Christian doctrine of suffering," is from C. S. Lewis, *The Problem of Pain* (New York: Macmillan, 1962), 115.

Chapter Eight — Arriving at the Final Questions

The quote that begins, "Most of us exist," is from Robert Macfarlane, *Mountains of the Mind* (New York: Pantheon, 2003), 274–275.

The quote that begins, "Why take a man," is from Catherine Marshall, *Light in My Darkest Night* (New York: Avon, 1989), 19.

The information on the Dust Bowl is from "NASA Explains 'Dust Bowl' Drought," posted on the Goddard Space Flight Center Web site: http://www.gsfc.nasa.gov/news-release/releases/2004/h04-095.htm (date of story: March 18, 2004). Information in the story comes from "On the Cause of the 1930s Dust Bowl," by Siegfried D. Schubert, Max J. Suarez, Philip J. Pegion, Randal D. Koster, and Julio T. Bacmeister in *Science*, 303 (2004), 1855–1859.

The quote that begins, "Do not be deceived," is from C. S. Lewis, *The Screwtape Letters* (New York: Macmillan, 1944; repr., West Chicago, Ill.: Lord and King, 1976), 51. Citations are to the Lord and King edition.

Chapter Nine — Surviving the Worst Day on the Mountain

The quote that begins, "tire-dump fire," is from Matt Dickinson, *The Other Side of Everest* (New York: Three Rivers, 1999), xvii.

The quote that begins, "Around 3:30 p.m.," is from Jon Krakauer, *Into Thin Air* (New York: Anchor/Doubleday, 1997), 246.

The quote that begins, "There, in the 'Death Zone,'" is from Dickinson, *Other Side of Everest*, xix.

Details from Rachel Scott's story are from Darrell Scott and Beth Nimmo with Steve Rabey, *Rachel's Tears* (Nashville: Thomas Nelson, 2000).

The quote that begins, "About four in the afternoon," is from Beck Weathers, "Dead Man Walking," in *The Mammoth Book of Eyewitness Everest*, ed. Jon E. Lewis (New York: Carroll and Graf, 2003), 391–392.

The quote that begins, "I couldn't believe what I saw," is from Lewis, *Eyewitness Everest*, 395.

The quote that begins, "It hurts me to see Beck," is from Krakauer, *Into Thin Air*, 368.

The quote that begins, "Somewhere in the midst," is from Lewis, *Eyewitness Everest*, 392–393.

The quote that begins, "Soon the people," is from Scott and Nimmo, *Rachel's Tears*, 21.

The quote that begins, "Dad, someday," is from Scott and Nimmo, *Rachel's Tears*, 21.

The quote that begins, "There was a numbness," is from Scott and Nimmo, *Rachel's Tears*, 22.

Chapter Ten – Realizing the Forces Pitted against Us

The quote that begins, "Not that I am," is from C. S. Lewis, *A Grief Observed* (New York: Seabury, 1961; repr., Bantam, 1976), 5. Citations are to the Bantam edition.

The quote that begins, "a wizard both cunning," is from J. R. R. Tolkien, *The Two Towers* (New York: Ballantine, 1966), 32.

The quote that begins, "Out of the wreck," is from J. R. R. Tolkien, *The Return of the King* (New York: Ballantine, 1966), 115.

The quote that begins, "'But,' said Sam," is from Tolkien, *Return of the King*, 337–338.

The quote that begins, "'I can't do this, Sam,'" is from the movie *The Two Towers*, directed by Peter Jackson, screenplay by Fran Walsh, Philippa Boyens, Stephen Sinclair, and Peter Jackson. A New Line Cinema Production, 2002.

The quote that begins, "'I see in your eyes,'" is from the movie *The Two Towers*, directed by Peter Jackson, screenplay by Fran Walsh, Philippa Boyens, and Peter Jackson. A New Line Cinema Production, 2003.

Glossary

The quote that begins, "The term 'Death Zone,'" is from Matt Dickinson, *The Other Side of Everest* (New York: Three Rivers, 1999), 7–8.

The quote that begins, "As a direct and indirect consequence," is from Dr. Oswald Otz, "Everest without Oxygen: The Medical Fundamentals," in *The Mammoth Book of Eyewitness Everest*, ed. Jon E. Lewis (New York: Carroll and Graf, 2003), 480–481.

The quote that begins, "The word *Sherpa* refers to a clan," is from Tashi Tenzing with Judy Tenzing, *Tenzing Norgay and the Sherpas of Everest* (New York: McGraw-Hill, 2001), xix, xxi.

The quote that begins, "A Sherpa boy looks up," is from Tenzing Norgay with James Ramsey Ullman, *Tiger of the Snows* (New York: Bantam, 1955), 76.

GLOSSARY

belay: To secure a climber with a rope, anchoring the climber with your weight.

col: A dip in a ridge or a mountain pass between two summits.

crampons: Steel spikes that are fitted to the sole of a climber's boots, used for gripping the ice and snow.

Cwm: (pronounced koom) — A valley formed by a glacier.

Death Zone: "The term 'Death Zone' was first coined in 1952 by Edouard Wyss-Dunant, a Swiss physician, in a book called *The Mountain World*. Drawing on the experiences of the Swiss Everest expedition of that year (which had so nearly made the summit), he described with remarkable accuracy the effects of altitude on the human body.

"Wyss-Dunant created a series of zones to help his readers understand. At the 6,000-meter (19,685-foot) zone, Wyss-Dunant concluded, it was still possible for the human body to acclimatize in the short term. At the 7,000-meter (22,965-foot) zone no acclimatization was possible.

"To the zone above 7,300 meters (23,950 feet), he gave a special name. He called it, in German, Todeszone, or Death Zone. Above that altitude, not only could human life not be sustained, it deteriorated with terrifying rapidity. Even using supplemental oxygen, no one can remain in the Death Zone for long.

"The term he invented is a uniquely chilling one, and one that sums up the sheer horror of a place in which every breath signals a deterioration of the human body, where the cells of vital organs are eliminated in their millions each hour, and where no living creature belongs.

"Like the 'Killing Fields,' the 'Death Zone,' in two simple words, carries with it a sense of unspeakable horror. It conjures up pictures of a place that might only have been imagined in the mind of a writer such as Tolkien: a place of quest in the medieval sense—a battle zone where warriors and dreamers come to fight the darkest forces of nature, and from which some men emerge so shaken by what they have experienced that they never find the strength to speak of it again."

edema: A leakage of blood from the capillaries. Edema may be cerebral or pulmonary. Cerebral edema occurs in the brain. Pulmonary edema occurs in the lungs.

hypoxia: Oxygen starvation in the tissues. "As a direct and indirect consequence of hypoxia, the symptom complex of acute mountain sickness develops. With milder forms the patient suffers from headaches, loss of appetite, nausea and vomiting. Sleep is disturbed and every form of activity becomes an exertion. One's mental capacity is reduced.

"Severe consequences of oxygen starvation include pulmonary edema, a concentration of water in the pulmonary vesicles which makes breathing more and more impossible, as well as cerebral edema, a tumor of the brain due to the increased water content of the brain cells."

icefall: The end of a glacier where ice breaks off in large and unstable chunks, sometimes the size of a house or a small office building. The Khumbu Icefall lies at the base of the Khumbu Glacier and is one of the most treacherous passages on Mount Everest.

Kathmandu: (pronounced kát-man-du) – The capital of Nepal.

piton: A metal pin that can be hammered into a rock or ice surface to form an anchor for a climber, or to run rope through.

scree: Small, loose rock.

Sherpa: "The word Sherpa refers to a clan of Tibetans who long lived in the southeastern reaches of Tibet, along the Himalayan border with Nepal, and most of whom migrated south into the high Nepalese valleys of the Solu Khumbu, stretching from Everest, starting between four and five hundred years ago. . . . In the early 1900s, as the Sherpas proved their great physical aptitude for Himalayan exploration and mountaineering, foreign sahibs began to use the term sherpa to refer to any high-altitude porter, or load-carrier."

Tenzing Norgay, the most acclaimed Sherpa, wrote this in his autobiography, which I thought a simple yet poignant observation, ripe for reflection: "A Sherpa boy looks up, and he sees a mountain. He looks down, and what does he see? A load. He picks up the load and starts for the mountain—or if not straight for it, at least up and down. It is not a strange or unpleasant thing for him, but a natural thing; and the load is not something to be handled awkwardly, to be struggled with and cursed at, but almost a part of his body."

traverse: To climb horizontally across a mountain.

Look for another
Tyndale book by Ken Gire

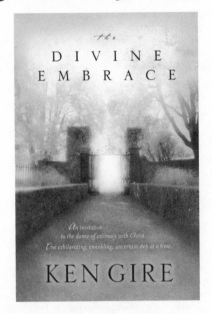

The Divine Embrace.
An invitation to the
dance of intimacy with Christ,
one exhilarating, ennobling,
uncertain step at a time.
Hardcover ISBN 0-8423-7023-4
Softcover ISBN 0-8423-7071-4